SCHOOL AMUSEMENTS;

OR,

How to make the School Interesting.

EMBRACING SIMPLE

RULES FOR MILITARY AND GYMNASTIC EXERCISES,

AND HINTS UPON THE

GENERAL MANAGEMENT OF THE SCHOOL ROOM.

With Engravings.

BY

N. W. TAYLOR ROOT.

NEW YORK:
A. S. BARNES & Co., 111 & 113 WILLIAM STREET,
(CORNER OF JOHN STREET.)

1869.

JONES & DENYSE,
Stereotypers and Electrotypers,
183 William-Street

PREFACE.

There are many teachers who think their business dull work, and who regret the necessity which compels them to continue in it. They undertook it only to make a little money, and they leave it, as soon as they can, for some other, and, as they think, more honorable, agreeable and lucrative employment.

There are other teachers who live somewhat away from the influences of modern improvements in the science, and who remain content to continue in the old-fashioned track of dull routine. Some of them, however, occasionally complain of the treadmill character of their daily toil, and wish, indefinitely, for some change.

A large proportion of our teachers are young and inexperienced. They are earnest and energetic; they are desirous of learning how to accomplish their duties fully and pleasantly; and they are thankful for any instruction in means and methods.

This book has been written for these three classes of teachers, and may prove of use to them. It is hoped, also, that almost every teacher may find something of value in it.

The writer has assumed, first, that teaching is *a business* as well as a profession, and that teachers not only *ought* to be, but *can* be pecuniarily successful. That which is called "business talent" among merchants is lamentably buried, generally, among teachers; for although in some parts of the country good salaries are paid to the teachers of public schools, and private schools are sometimes successful enterprises, yet it cannot be denied that a large majority of the teachers of the land are poor, and remain poor. We hear very rarely of fortunes made at teaching, or even of salaries paid which are not less than those which "smart" clerks receive in trade. Business maxims and shrewdness, and enterprise, are not carried into the trade of teaching, and until they are, teaching will be a "poor business."

Teachers must learn to imitate, in some respects, the practices of "business men." Among them "capital" does not always control success, but advertising and attractive display, and "bargains" offered and "inducements" held out, and winning courtesy and industry, energy, and a little Yankee shrewdness—these, when combined, seldom fail to gain custom and profit.

Investing money, even some of his hard-earned dollars, in organizing a company, or in fitting up a gymnasium, may be for the teacher what advertising has been for many a successful merchant. Time devoted to teaching, as a business, out of school, during vacations, constantly, may be rewarded with a success equal to that of our "devoted business men." It is very well to say that if a school or a business is worthy of success, it will have it in due time without "puffing," if you can afford, or are willing to wait; but if you have not the capital of reputation, push your business, gain a deserved popularity, and *achieve* success.

Far be it from the writer to advise deceit, humbug, or quackery in this noble profession; these are as unnecessary and unwise as they are censurable. It is believed that the various plans recommended in this volume will be found to be worthy of adoption by honest teachers, and that they offer real advantages to teachers, parents, and scholars. They certainly are not proposed as mere "tricks of the trade."

A second point assumed is, that teaching may be made a more pleasant occupation than it usually is. That teacher who communicates with his scholars only from his desk, as "the master;" who never unbends his dignified authority, nor relaxes his strict discipline, but maintains ever the state of a monarch, and surrounds himself with a hedge of enforced respect; who neither knows nor cares to learn of any means by which school-labor may be made cheerful and attractive, and never attempts to remove the natural repugnance which children have for abstract mental effort; such a teacher can never *enjoy* teaching. But it *may* be made a "delightful task" Some of the writer's happiest hours have been spent in his school-room, or among his scholars out of school; and the remembrance of the many acts of kindness and evidences of affection which they have done and shown, will brighten the whole of his life. Teaching is a *noble* profession, and the true teacher is one of the most useful, and may be one of the happiest, of men.

To those who desire to teach more profitably or more pleasantly, or both, the following pages are offered, with the belief that they will not be found without some worth. The book is not a compilation of theories, but the result of practical experience. It contains no plan which has not been thoroughly tried and found useful. It might, undoubtedly, be a better book, and criticisms which may be made with the design of aiding the cause which the writer advocates, are desired rather than deprecated. He wishes, however, to shield himself from a charge which may be made, that he advises *too much* amusement. It may be remembered that the subject written upon is *only* "School Amusements," and that these exercises are offered as suitable to be *joined to labor*, or *thrown around it as a disguise*. The writer would have, indeed, gained little from experience, if he had not learned that nothing can be accomplished without labor, *hard* labor; but he thinks that he has also learned that some, if not all kinds of work may be made to *seem play*.

In conclusion, this addition is made to the volumes of "The Teacher's Library," with the hope that it may not be unworthy of at least the last place there; and to hear that any of his fellow-teachers are pleased with, and aided by, its perusal, will be a rich reward to

THE AUTHOR.

CONTENTS.

EVERY TEACHER HIS OWN DRILL-MASTER.

GYMNASTICS.

SCHOOL MANAGEMENT.

EVERY TEACHER

HIS OWN DRILL-MASTER.

INTRODUCTION.

MILITARY organizations in boys' schools have become popular, not only in the Eastern States, but in many other parts of the country, and this in spite of many objections which were at first raised against them, both by parents and teachers. It has been proved by experiment, in some of our best, our *model* schools, that the objections to the system are by no means well-founded, and, on the other hand, that the advantages arising from its adoption are many and real.

One of the objections to such organizations has been, that they would tend to foster a warlike and belligerent spirit; would lead boys to become, when men,

> Full of strange oaths,
> Jealous in honor, sudden and quick in quarrel,
> Seeking the bubble reputation,
> Even in the cannon's mouth."

"If," says the editor of the Ohio Journal of Education, in the May issue for the last year, "if this objection is well-founded, it should be fatal to all such enterprises. We certainly ought not to adopt the Spartan policy, and imbue the minds of our sons with a taste for blood and carnage. But we are not of those who have faith in the justice of this objection. Properly managed, such exercises can have no influence so to deprave the heart and vitiate the morals, as to fit one for the employment of fighting. Even participation in wars does not generally promote a desire for war. The most distinguished warriors are, many times, the most ardent friends of peace. Such was Washington, such is Scott."

In addition to this theoretical answer to the objection, it may be urged that actual experiment has, in no instance which has come under the notice of many teachers who have conferred on the subject, developed such Spartan tastes as have been feared; on the contrary, cases may be cited where boys, who had been longing to enter the Academy at West Point, have expressed themselves contented with military experience, as acquired at school.

Another objection has been, that the expense of such organizations must be very considerable, too great, indeed, for many, if not most, parents to bear.

In reply it may be said that, "in some instances this may be true, where costly uniform and accoutrements are prescribed. But this need never be. The uniform required may be as cheap and plain as any other decent apparel; and as for arms, they can generally be provided without subjecting the indigent to expense, or they can be dispensed with, and *lances* used, the cost of which would be next to nothing."—*Ohio Journal of Education.*

Boys are content with but little finery in the way of gold lace and feathers; at least this has been the experience of the writer and other teachers of his acquaintance.

In the concluding chapter of this section, the subject of uniform is dwelt upon at length, and it is shown that the objection of expense amounts to nothing at all, if, as is claimed, there are any real advantages to be derived from the system.

The advantages claimed are these:

1. Habits of *promptness*, *exactness*, and *unanimity* of *action*, are fostered, and very generally confirmed.

2. *Subordination* is taught and practised. Implicit obedience to command, without "grumbling" or questioning, is necessarily a distinguishing characteristic of military discipline, and it is just this which boys, now-a-days, need to learn.

3. *Erectness* of *carriage*, a *regard* for a *neat* and *clean appearance*, and *gentlemanly* and *respectful behavior;* these are taught, and not only *taught*, but by enforcement *learned.*

4. An *attraction* is *added* to *the school.* This is an important point. It is to collect and present to teach-

ers tried and approved attractions to the school-house, which is the object of this book, and it is the writer's opinion, and that of many teachers, as the result of experience, that hardly any other more real and worthy attraction than this can be found.

5. Time is occupied by the drilling, parading, planning, and talking, consequent on the adoption of a military organization, which might, and probably would, be spent in amusements more or less vicious and hurtful.

If amusements are not provided for children, they will make them for themselves, and all know that the tendency of the usual amusements and conversation of boys is, unfortunately, towards vulgarity and even wickedness. But boys are never unwilling to submit to the direction of a parent or teacher, who, in a friendly and sympathizing spirit, proposes such amusements as the one under discussion, or as those indicated in the chapter on "Gymnastics." Indeed, it may be confidently relied upon that not a single boy will be at all unwilling to "play soger."

The success attending the adoption of the military plan at several popular schools is a final argument in its favor. Among these may be mentioned the "Collegiate and Commercial Institute," conducted by Dr Russell, at New Haven, Ct., and "The Rectory School," by Rev. Mr. Everest, at Hampden, Ct. With both of these the writer is well acquainted. To these may be added the large and celebrated school at Sing Sing, N. Y., the public schools at Zanesville and Toledo, Ohio, and many others, in various places at the North and East.

The writer, who has been, for several years, a successful teacher, has had considerable experience in the initiation and continuation of military exercises in his own school, and has thought that his brother teachers might be pleased to examine, and perhaps adopt, the system of organization and drilling which follows.

His authorities in regard to "first principles" are, mainly, the regular army instructions, as taught in his school by an ex-captain of the Mexican war, and as contained in "Scott's Tactics."

It is hoped that the instructions here given will be sufficiently plain to enable every teacher to become his own drill-master; yet it is advised that where a competent instructor can be procured, he be employed. In many cases this will be difficult or impossible, and perhaps, with this guide, it may be unnecessary.

The writer would add, that he will be happy at all times to answer letters of inquiry from teachers on points not made sufficiently clear in the following chapters. Direct to him, through the Publishers.

TO THE TEACHER.

I MAY be excused for adopting, hereafter, a familiar style, one in which I may *talk* freely to my reader. Let me address you, my brother-teacher, as familiarly as I should be glad to do, could I meet you personally, and talk over with you my plans of drilling and organization.

Much depends on presenting the subject properly to your boys. It will not do to *force* the matter upon them, nor even to let it seem too much your own plan. Start the ball by asking them, rather carelessly, how they would like "to get up a company;" say that you have just met with a book of instructions in drilling, and that perhaps you can teach them how to march and "shoulder arms," just like real soldiers. Let this leaven work, and, in a few days, they will be urging you to organize and drill them.

You must consult your own judgment as to whether you should or should not talk of the matter with the parents of your scholars. If you are independent of trustees, or similar control, and are confident of your standing with your patrons, you may well go on without consulting them. They will become convinced in time of the merits of the plan. I speak here from experience.

But if you are under control, you will do well to let slip the plan among your boys *before* consulting with "the powers that be;" for you will then be sure of their influence, besides your own, in favor of the proposition.

We will suppose that the matter is decided on, and that the boys have talked it over among themselves, and with their parents, and are now urging you to go on.

Call a meeting after school, some afternoon, to consider the question, "Shall we have a company?" At this meeting, after talking of all the possibilities in favor of the plan, remark to them that there is one *difficulty* in the way, one that you are really afraid of, but one that, after all, depends on them for its removal. *Ready* and *entire obedience* is a *sine quâ non* in soldiering. (Let me talk to your boys myself.)

"If the captain orders his men to march to the right, and some of them prefer to go to the left, what becomes of the company? Or if he commands, 'shoulder arms,' and some would rather 'Fire,' and do so, would *that* be doing right? And suppose again that I, as your captain, order a drill for some afternoon, and some half-dozen or so of you stay away; but at that drill the company learns a new exercise, and at the next drill, they who staid away, of course, do not know this exercise, and by their awkwardness, 'put out' all the rest, and throw the company into confusion.

"Now how can we avoid such troubles as these? This is the way I propose: Let every one who joins the company promise to obey me and the other officers in every particular, without a 'why' or a 'wherefore,' an 'if' or a 'but.' If you will promise me this, I will go on and do all that I can to help you become a fine company; and when we are well enough drilled, we will make a public parade."

It will be well for you to draw up a kind of pledge of obedience to all your martial orders, and require them to sign it, so that they may be influenced by the consciousness of having given a distinct and individual promise to obey.

And here will be the place to connect the company with the school, by declaring that bad boys, or bad scholars, shall not belong to the company. You can do this, or not, as you think best. I can only say that I have not found such a course necessary.

After having secured their promise to obey, you can appoint a drill for some future time, as soon as may be, requiring only, in the way of uniform, that they all wear jackets and caps. If they ask about uniform, arms, or drums, remark that they must leave all that to you for awhile, and that you will report to them as soon as you have decided on anything.

You may consult the chapter on "Uniform, &c.;" and be in no hurry, for you will have no need of any of these things for several weeks.

In preparation for your first, and every drill, you must have thoroughly studied and practised every movement which you are to teach. Do not carry the book with you to the parade-ground. When on the ground, assume a martial bearing. It will be well for the success of your plan that your dress be somewhat *a la militaire;* carry, also, a light cane, as an officer would carry a sword. Consult the drill on "sword exercise," and employ the "carry arms," while drilling. In demeanor be energetic, prompt and decided; use no waste words, and err, if at all, on the side of severity, rather than of familiarity. In fine, become an example of a soldier to them, in every respect.

DRILL FIRST.

The drill master assumes, himself, "the position of the soldier," in front of the "line" he wishes to form, and says:

"Boys! the command that I shall give you, pretty soon, will be, *Squad!* FALL IN! I will explain this:—it means, make a line, side by side, facing me; not too close to each other: without crowding; as you come up, don't crowd in at the centre of the line, but seek a place at the left, next to the last man; above all, fall in without talking or laughing, or even smiling." The drill master repeats these instructions, very distinctly and emphatically.

Squad!—FALL IN!

"Remember the instructions I gave you. *No talking!* Let your arms hang naturally at your sides, the middle finger of each hand just touching the seam of your trowsers; stand only so near your neighbor on either side that your elbows, while remaining in that position, shall touch, but not press, their elbows. If you are crowded, move a little toward the left; and if you feel pressure from your right-hand man, you must move toward the left." The drill master takes care that the line is neither crowded nor too thin. "Now, turn your heads (not your shoulders) towards the right of the line, and look along the line to see if you are not too far forward or behind: if forward, fall back; if behind, come forward. Nothing looks worse in a company than crooked lines; we must pay particular attention to this.

"My next command will be, *Squad!*—ATTENTION! You are not to move until you hear the last word, but then you are to face to the front; heads stiff on your shoulders, with the chin drawn in; eyes not looking at me, but on the ground, about twelve paces in front of you; arms hanging as I directed before; chests thrown forward, not the stomachs." The drill master illustrates, personally, the difference between protruding the chest and the abdomen, giving them a side view of each.

"Heels together, with the weight of the body resting on both feet; toes turned out equally, so that the two feet shall make one exact letter V. Try this now, and be ready for the command,

"*Squad!*—ATTENTION!"

The drill master takes particular pains with each one to see that he now obeys the directions, in every one of these particulars. He gives as much praise and encouragement as possible.

"This, boys, is 'the position of the soldier,' as it is called. It is the position which you are always to take at the command, 'attention,' and one which you are to retain, with but little change, while 'under arms.' Try, each one, to think over every particular; the position of the *head*, *eyes*, *chest*, *arms*, *hands*, *legs*, and *feet*. Let your heads be as stiff on your shoulders, as if you had swallowed a poker. Let's see how long you can retain that position. Remember that I have taught you two commands: 'Squad! Fall in!' and 'Squad! Attention!' I shall dismiss you now, for a recess, and shall call you together again in a few minutes." The drill master reviews, briefly, the explanations of each command, and then says:

"DISMISSED!"

During the recess, the drill master drills the awkward ones individually, advising all to look on. He takes "the position" himself, and asks them to observe the positions of his head, eyes, chest, and limbs. After a short recess he commands,

"*Squad!*—FALL IN!"

The drill master uses but few explanations. The only trouble here will be found in their crowding into the line. If this is serious, the drill master may insist on each one falling in on the left of the line. This is the rule, always. Be sure to get the line as straight as possible.

"*Squad!*—ATTENTION!"

"Let each one of you remember the explanations. Take 'the position' in every respect. Think of your *heads*, *eyes*, *chest*, *arms*, *hands*, *legs*, and *feet*. Remain just so, while I talk a little while.

"Perhaps you think this rather dull work. You hoped to have guns on your shoulders, and to go marching around the play-ground at this very first drill. But think a moment. You couldn't walk until you had learned to creep; you couldn't read until you had learned to spell. Some of you didn't learn to spell *well*, and now what kind of readers and writers are you? We are now learning the *alphabet* of soldiering, and I hope you are content to go slowly and surely." The drill master makes other similar remarks. If there has been talking in the ranks, he makes a particular law against it, and reminds them of their promise to obey him.

With one more dismissal, and calls to "fall in," and the order "attention,"—and this third time without *any* explanation,—he closes the drill.

DRILL SECOND.

"*Squad!*—FALL IN! *Squad!*—ATTENTION!"

Let there be a careful review of previous drill. "You will have observed, boys, that these commands are in two parts. The first part is called 'the word of caution,' the second 'the word of execution.' I will illustrate this. The next command will be, *Eyes*—RIGHT! 'The word of caution' is, 'Eyes.' You are warned by that word that something is to be done with the eyes. You are to *do* nothing until you hear 'the word of execution,' which is, 'Right.' As soon as you hear that, you are to turn your heads toward the right, so far that the left eye shall be on a line with the buttons of your jacket, and are to glance along the line toward the right. You are to remain in this position until you hear the command, 'Front,' when you are to resume the first position. Now we will try it.

"*Eyes*—RIGHT."

The drill master corrects such errors as heads turned too much or poked forward. He reminds them of the poker, which *never* allows the head to assume any other than an upright position.

"FRONT!"

"*Eyes*—RIGHT! FRONT! *Eyes*—RIGHT! FRONT!'

Repeat these several times. If they are not well done, the drill master may stand at the right of the line, and remark, "Boys, I want this motion done by all at precisely the same instant. Let the heads move just as if there were a long wire running through all the noses, and I should jerk it this way, at the word 'Right.'

The drill master's voice, in giving a command, must be very decided in tone. Utter "the word of caution" rather slowly. Make a sufficient pause, but not too long, between the words, and *jerk out* the last word and *bite off the end* of it, a few tones higher than that in which the first word was pronounced.

"Eyes—left!" is performed as the reverse of the previous command. The drill master drills them for some time on both, never forgetting that "Front!" must follow each command.

"One object, boys, of these exercises, is to teach you to move together. The beauty of all military maneuvres consists in exact harmony and oneness of the execution of the commands. And the only way by which this perfection can be attained is this: Each man must listen attentively to every order, and at the very instant he hears the last word, he must execute it thoroughly. I say *thoroughly*, because, if one turns his head, in 'Eyes right' or 'Eyes left,' as he ought, and the next one turns only his *eyes*, there will be an imperfect line.

"My next command will be 'Right—Dress!' At the last word, you will do just as you did in 'Eyes—Right;' and, in addition to that, you will immediately correct your position in line. If you are too far forward of the rest, you will fall back quietly, until you are so placed as to see no further up the line than the buttons on the coat of the third man from you: if you are behind the line, you will come forward and find the same place. Thus you will make the line straight. Of course, the right-hand man stands fast, although he turns his head like the rest. Besides this, if you find you are at too great a distance from your right-hand man, take side steps toward him, until your elbow just touches his. Now we will try it.

"*Right*—DRESS!"

The drill master stands at the right of the line, and orders particular individuals to come forward, or fall back, as may be necessary.

"FRONT!"

The drill master may observe that some are forgetting "the position," and, in rather a stern voice, he orders,

"ATTENTION!"

and reminds them of their forgetfulness. "Left dress" is the converse of "Right dress." "Front" follows each command. The drill master drills them in both.

"Rest" is performed by bringing the hands together, the left crossed over the right; arms at full length; left foot brought at right angles with the line; right foot thrown back, the hollow three inches in the rear of the heel of the left foot, and parallel with the line; weight of the body on the right foot. See plate No. 1.

The command "Attention" brings them back to "the position."

"Break ranks—March!" is performed by clapping the hands together briskly once, and leaving ranks for a recess or dismissal.

The drill master will practise both of these, taking care to have them well done, and then will close the drill, after a recess, with,

"*Squad!*—FALL IN! ATTENTION!
Eyes—RIGHT! FRONT!
Eyes—LEFT! FRONT!
REST! ATTENTION!
Right—DRESS! FRONT!
Left—DRESS! FRONT!
REST! ATTENTION!
Break ranks—MARCH!"

A drill should rarely extend beyond an hour.

REMARKS.

If reviews are necessary, as they probably will be, the third drill may be entirely a review.

The teacher will need to guard against,

1st. Talking and playing, "sky-larking," as it is termed, in ranks. This *must* be checked, and, if possible, entirely prevented; because the *whole* attention of the soldier should be given to the commands. If, while practising, "Eyes Right," and "Eyes Left," or "Right Dress," and "Left Dress," a boy is playing, and fails to observe "the word of caution," he will be likely to make a mistake; others, thinking that he is right and they wrong, will follow him; the neighbors will laugh, and be unprepared for the next order. This is only an illustration; the principle applies to the whole course of drilling. Explain all this to your boys, and obtain their conviction to the necessity of this, your strictest law. Bring penalties to bear, if necessary.

2d. Forgetfulness concerning "the position of a soldier." It may be safely said, that if, by any means, the teacher can secure attention and correctness in this particular, he may be sure of having a well-drilled company, in every respect. If the boys can be induced to pay sufficient attention to their work to maintain "the position" strictly and continually, they may be relied on for accuracy in all other particulars. It is the A B C of discipline.

3d. A desire to advance too rapidly in learning new movements. "Slow and sure" *must* be the motto at the commencement. The teacher must insist on accuracy on the part of all and each. These "first principles," as they are called, must be practised over and over again. At every drill, a review of the previous drills must be gone through with, and nothing new learned until all that has been taught before is perfectly acquired. Yet the teacher must avoid fatiguing his troops. He must give all the variety possible. He must also avoid harshness and severity. He should drill an "awkward squad" by itself, making it something of a disgrace to be ranked in this corps.

Finally, the teacher must, above all, be himself all that he desires his soldiers to become.

DRILL THIRD.

"REST!" In this position, hereafter, give all explanations; none while under the command, "Attention."

"*Right*—FACE," is performed by throwing the weight of the body on the left foot, making the heel of that foot the pivot on which the body turns, the right foot being raised very slightly and brought around, while turning, to the V position, the one employed always while the soldier is not in motion. (See plate No. 1.)

These "facings" are rather difficult. The drill master needs to practise them himself to perfection, before attempting to teach them.

"In turning, be careful not to sway the body nor bend the knees. Do not move with a jerk. When faced to the right, the man in front of you is called your 'file-leader'; look him right in the back of the neck."

The drill master will now give "Right face" three times in succession, when the line will be again facing him. He must caution them to keep their heads up, and to pay continual attention to "the position."

Before giving "Left face,"—which is done in the same way with "Right face,"—the drill master will remark:

"Observe, boys, that 'the word of caution' tells you in which direction you are to face. As soon as you hear the word 'Right,' or 'Left,' *think* towards the right, or left, of the line. If you give the attention you ought, there can be no excuse for you if you face the wrong way."

In these facings, the drill master will observe that if the line is crowded, there is trouble in turning, on account of collisions. He may obviate this by giving a "right dress." Definition:—Heads turned so that the left eye is on a line with the buttons, and not poked forward; eyes glanced along the line so that the fourth man is invisible; and now, particularly, position taken so that elbows only just touch neighboring elbows. "No crowding or ill-feeling if a right-hand man presses you; yield to pressure from that side, if a 'right dress' is given; the reverse, if 'left dress.'—'Front,' *always* follows a 'dress.'"

The execution of these facings, together with a thorough review of previous lessons, ought to occupy the time of this drill. But, for a novelty, the drill master may prepare for "sizing."

Let some contrivance be prepared by which the stature of every boy may be determined. Each one should be furnished with a card, on which should be marked, distinctly, his feet and inches of height, so that he may remember them. The card has, also, other future uses.

DRILL FOURTH.

Before falling in, let each one have his card pinned on his back, just below the collar. After the line is formed (by *Squad*—FALL IN! ATTENTION! *Right*—DRESS! FRONT!) give command, "*Right*—FACE! *Size*—MARCH!" At this, each boy who sees a lower figure than his own in front of him, takes a side step to the right and advances until he sees a higher number, when he steps again into file; and each boy who sees a higher number endeavoring to come in front of him, quietly falls back.

When all have found places, require them to notice who their file-leaders are, so as to remember them, and thus make the next sizing less difficult. Require also a distance of sixteen inches from back to chest, (which is *always* to be preserved in file,) for convenience in coming to the front. The order to secure this is, "Take your fronting distance." They may easily understand how much space to allow, by your remarking that there should be just room enough between each man, in file, for another man to slip into, with a close fit. At the words, "Take your fronting distance," they who are too near their file-leaders must fall back, but never *crowd* back.

The teacher must observe that in dealing with boys, he must be continually on the watch against talking and playing in ranks. There will, probably, be some of this in sizing, some disputing about places. Every means should be adopted to repress this entirely.

The squad is now "in file," facing towards the right. "FRONT," brings them into line. If the line is crooked, give, "Right—dress."

"*Mark time*—MARCH!" At the word of caution, the weight of the body rests on the right foot; the left foot is held ready to take a step. At the word "March," the left foot is thrown forward, as if to advance, and brought back to place: the right foot follows in the same way. There is no advancing, and care must be taken to bring the feet back into their tracks, or the line will be broken. While "marking time," the drill master counts "one, two,—one, two,—one, two," &c., in slow time, a little less than seconds.

The command, "*Squad*—HALT!" stops them. The word "halt" must *always* be given *just as either foot strikes the ground;* there will then follow one more motion of the other foot, which all will bring down together, and cease marking time.

The drill master must repeat the explanations of "marking time," and "halting," very distinctly. They must learn to rest the body on the right foot at the first word, and to throw out the left foot at the word "march." Insist that the body shall not be allowed to sway about while marking time; that the head shall be kept erect; that the eyes be all directed to the front, striking the ground twelve paces off; and that the arms and hands be held correctly. The drill master must be prepared to give illustrations, himself, of marking time and halting; and, to stimulate ambition, he may command a "Rest," select half-a-dozen or more of his best soldiers, form them in line, facing the rest, and drill them as an example.

Schedule of orders in review, to close this drill:

After a "Break Ranks—March!"

"*Squad!*—FALL IN!
ATTENTION!
Right—FACE!
Size—MARCH!—FRONT!
Right—DRESS!—FRONT!
Eyes—RIGHT!—FRONT!
Eyes—LEFT!—FRONT!
Right—FACE!—FRONT!
Left—FACE!—FRONT!
REST!—ATTENTION!
Left—DRESS!—FRONT!
Mark Time—MARCH!
Squad—HALT!
Right—FACE!—FRONT!
Break ranks—MARCH!"

These orders (varied at pleasure, and given promptly, so that they are kept at work actively) will give a good review.

Interest will be added to the affair if visitors are present, especially military visitors, ladies, sweethearts, and parents.

2*

DRILL FIFTH.

REVIEW, ESPECIALLY "THE FACINGS."

"*About*—FACE!" Consult plate No. 1. At the word "About," the position of the "Rest" is assumed with the feet, (eyes, in both orders, to the front;) at the word "Face," turn, on the left heel, completely around, bringing the right foot to the side of the left; the line will then be faced so that their backs are toward the drill master. To "make the motion *tell*," so that the executions of the order may be simultaneous, it will be well to require a *stamp* of the right foot as it is brought back, at the word "About." Do not go on to order "Face," until "About" is well learned. To recover first position, when "About" is imperfectly performed, give, "*Bring back right foot at two; one*—TWO!"

Require avoidance of jostling each other in turning; let them move as easily as possible. Drill some of the best, as examples, in front of the line. Illustrate frequently yourself. This "about face" is a difficult motion. Be patient; spend much time on it, at this and subsequent drills. Critics will watch this motion on parade.

Continue with, "*Mark time*—MARCH! *Squad*—HALT! *Right*—FACE!" You may now try marking time "in file." Require all to lift and throw forward the left foot first, and at the same instant. There will be no kicking of heels if all move together. If there are collisions, repress hard feelings, kindly.

Practise marking time in file a long time, promising them that as soon as they do this well, they shall march. While marking time, give, "*Forward*—MARCH!" taking care to pronounce the word "march" as the right feet strike the ground. Marching, either from marking time or from a halt, must be by "*the left foot first.*" Let them march only a few paces at a time. "Squad—halt," stops them. Require that they keep their "fronting distance" while marching in file. If any one finds himself getting behind, he must take longer steps. "*Lengthen the pace, but never lose the time.*" While marching by file, if you wish to turn to the right or left, command "*File*—RIGHT!" or "*File*—LEFT!" This order is obeyed by the file-leader, the one who stands on the extreme right, "in line." (If, however, the company is marching "by the left flank, file right or left," the left-hand man is file leader.) He turns promptly to the right or left, and the rest follow him. To prevent their making "rounded corners," stand yourself at the angle, and require them to march fully up to the corner, before turning. Take care to secure "square corners."

The pace which is taken while turning is necessarily a short one, and as they who have passed the corner are advancing at the usual pace, ground will be lost by the one turning, unless he remembers to *lengthen the pace two steps after passing the angle.* This is an important point. It will be difficult for them, if frequent turns are made, to keep fronting distance. To demonstrate this, give, suddenly, while they are marching in file, "*Squad*—HALT!" (Remember where and when to utter that word "halt.") You will find them straggling along at unequal distances. Call them to a "front," and give a "right dress!" Tell them that they *must* remember to preserve, while marching, the exact "fronting distance."

They must always look their file-leaders in the back of the neck.

They must carry their arms without swinging, and yet not as if pinioned to their sides.

They must remember *the poker*.

Close this drill, after a recess, with

"*Squad*—FALL IN!	*Right*—FACE!
ATTENTION!	*Size*—MARCH!—FRONT!
Right—DRESS!—FRONT!	*Break ranks*—MARCH!"

DRILL SIXTH.

After the line is formed and sized in the usual manner, command, "*Tell off in odd and even numbers, commencing on the right,—tell* OFF!" Right-hand man counts "one," at the same time jerking his head towards the left, as in the order, "Eyes left;" his head resumes position to the front as soon as the word is uttered. Next man counts "two," third man, "one," fourth, "two," and so on; all turning the head. It is desirable that all observe a certain tone in counting, as nearly similar as is possible with boys' voices. The rhythm of this counting should be in half seconds.

If any one fails to turn his head, or counts wrong, order "*Stop counting!*" and begin again. Go back a dozen times, if necessary, but never allow an error. Tell each man to remember his number; and then give, "*odd numbers stand fast, even numbers an oblique step to the right and rear*—MARCH!" Each of the even numbers (the "two's,") will take a backward step with his right foot in such a way (obliquely) as to bring him directly in the rear of the one who was his right-hand man; he is to make but one step of it; the right foot must be thrown backwards and sideways at the same time, the left foot following, and making at once the usual V with the right. The squad will then be in double file, (in two rows,) the "two's" all directly behind the "one's," and they should stand at rather more than the usual "fronting distance" in the rear of the "one's."

If the motion is not well done, give, "*Into line*—MARCH!" The two's (the rear rank) start with the left foot and, at one step, resume their places in line. Try this again and repeatedly, until they can do it well.

Since, at the next drill, on account of absences, some of the "one's" may be "two's," change your command to, "*Even* numbers stand fast, *odd* numbers an oblique step to the right and rear—*march!*"

When all have well learned this, give, "*Ranks, right and left*,—FACE!" At this order, the *front rank* faces to the *right*, the *rear rank* to the *left*. Be particular here: caution them against being confused. If they blunder at this, "Front!" will bring them back for another trial.

Now order, "*Form company*—MARCH!" The right-hand man of the front rank will come to the front, the remainder of this rank will march up to him and come to the front on his line, and the rear rank will file right, and right again, and march on, following the example of the front rank.

Perhaps you will be obliged to take one rank at a time. There will be no difficulty with the front rank, for their duty is simple: they will close up in file and come to the front as each man reaches his place. Let the drill master then go to the rear rank and order "*File right*—MARCH! *File right again!*" Bring the head of the column nearly up to the left of the front rank, and order, "*Rear rank*—HALT!" Time the order so that they shall halt at the right place, close to the left of the front rank. Then give, "FRONT! *Squad—Right*—DRESS! FRONT!" and the thing is done. When they have once done this they will not forget it.

You now have the taller boys at the extremes, and the shorter ones at the centre of the line.

Command, "*Tell off in whole numbers, commencing on the right*—TELL OFF!" The counting now is "one, two, three, four," and so on, to the left. The head is turned as in the previous counting, and the rhythm and tone attended to. Make them perfect in this also.

We will suppose that you have twenty-four boys, all told. You can divide them now into four sections, of six each. Command, "*Tell off in sections of six, commencing on the right*—TELL OFF!" The count is now, "one, two, three, four, five, six,—one, two, three, four, five, six,—one, two, three, four, five, six,—one, two, three, four, five, six." Each number "one" is "the right" of his section, each "six" is "the left."

Go to each "one" and each "six" and say, "You are the right (or left) of the 2d (or other) section: you must not get into any other."

Command, "*First section stand fast; second, third, and fourth sections, left*—FACE! *Prove distance,*—MARCH!" At this order, the second section marches forward toward the left *two* paces, the third section *four* paces, and the fourth section *six* paces. They halt there, and the order then is, to them, "Front!" Now your sections are in line, as before, but there is a space of two paces between the left and right of each section. These spaces are for officers, when they shall have been appointed.

By this arrangement your taller boys constitute the first and fourth sections, and the shorter ones are all in the second and third; that is, they are at the centre of the company.

You will have occupied the whole hour, and perhaps more, by these maneuvres. Close by "REST!" during which you call a company meeting, for the next afternoon, for election of officers; they have sections and need sergeants.

"ATTENTION! *Break ranks*—MARCH!"

Note.—In these instructions for dividing your company into sections, I supposed, for the sake of simplicity, that there were twenty-four in line. There may not often be less, but there may frequently be more. For instance, there may be twenty-eight, thirty-two, thirty-six, or any number divisible by four. In such a case, take one-fourth of the whole number,—say thirty-two,—and command them to tell off in sections of (say) eight. But suppose that there is a number not divisible by four, in line,—as twenty-five,—there must then be an odd number in one of the sections. Command then, "*Tell off in sections of* (say) *six, commencing at the second file*—TELL OFF! "The second file," means the second man from the right. You now have seven in the first section, and six in each of the others.

Suppose you had twenty-six. The same order will apply to this case also, as you will find on trial; you will have seven in the first and fourth sections, and six in each of the others.

It may happen that the taller boys are more numerous than the short ones, in which case it will be well to add to the numbers of the second and third sections, rather than to those of the first and fourth.

REMARKS.

I will suppose that your company consists of at least thirty-one members. You will need three "commissioned officers," four sergeants, and four corporals. I will speak of these officers in order of rank:

1. CAPTAIN,—who should be one of the oldest boys; one who has been conspicuous, in drill, for attention and a certain quickness in apprehending and executing commands, and one who is a favorite among his fellows. To him you will resign the command, in time.

2. 1ST LIEUTENANT,—who must possess, as nearly as possible, the requisites desirable in a captain. He is vice-captain, and may succeed him. He has command of the "first platoon," and his commands take precedence of those of the sergeants.

3. 2D LIEUTENANT,—who must also resemble the captain. He has command of the "second platoon," and his orders, also, are to be received as from the third in authority. The soldier's rule is, "Obey the highest authority you have given you."

If you find three boys who are pretty nearly alike in capacity and popularity, you will do well to allow the company to elect, from them, their three highest officers.

4. 1st, or Orderly Sergeant,—who must, like all other officers, have capacity and popularity. He commands the "first section," and should be chosen from that section. He is also the secretary of the company. keeps and calls "the roll," musters and forms the company, (as shown hereafter,) and is, in some respects, a most important officer.

5. 2d Sergeant,—who has command only of "second section," which is one of the two short ones. He should be chosen from his section.

6. 3d Sergeant,—is to be chosen as the 2d sergeant, and commands only his section.

7. 4th Sergeant,—should be chosen from the "fourth section," which he commands.

8. 1st Corporal; 9. 2d Corporal; 10. 3d Corporal; 11. 4th Corporal.—These corporals have no commands. They are merely "guides of company," stationed at the left of their respective sections. They carry guns, (the other officers all carry swords,) and drill as privates. They should be chosen for eminent soldierly behavior, steadiness, and attention.

You will be prepared now to appoint and elect your officers. At the next drill I will show their positions, and more particular duties.

These are all the officers necessary, even if your company numbers forty or fifty. But if you have less than thirty-one, you may appoint one captain, four lieutenants, each commanding a section, and four corporals. Rather than do this, I would advise you to endeavor to fill up your corps with boys not belonging to your school. However, sections of five, including corporals, will "*do*," and if you have only twenty-seven in all, you can have the seven officers first mentioned.

At this meeting, called to elect officers, you should complete a regular company organization. Your constitution and by-laws may be at present brief and unfinished; circumstances will teach you what laws are necessary, such as fines or other penalties for absence from drill, disobedience of orders, talking in ranks, &c., &c.; but your boys should go through the formality of signing some kind of instrument, which shall bind them to good conduct.

The "orderly" must prepare a roll of names, (not including commissioned officers,) in alphabetical order, with spaces to mark absences, &c.

A company name must be chosen. After suggesting a few appropriate names, ("——— Cadets," is a good one,) you might allow balloting

DRILL SEVENTH.

At this drill, and hereafter, "the orderly" forms the company, as has been shown in the two previous drills. You will need to instruct him thoroughly in his duties before going on the ground, and should prompt him while he is giving his orders. His orders and movements are as follows:

He is to stand at "1ˢ" (see plate No. 2,) and to command, "*Cadets*—FALL IN!" (At this word the captain and lieutenants take the places assigned to them in the plate: the 2d, 3d and 4th sergeants, and the four corporals, form in line, in the rear. The 2d sergeant has command of this temporary line, and may order "Right dress," &c., if necessary.) "ATTENTION!" He now calls "the roll," and marks absences—each one responding, "Present," on hearing his name. "*Right*—DRESS! FRONT! *Right*—FACE!" (If any of these motions are not well done, he must repeat them.) "*Size*—MARCH!" (He cautions, "*Get your fronting distance!*") "FRONT! *Right*—DRESS!" (A line not straight, *perfectly* straight, ought to be an eye-sore to any officer.) "FRONT! *Tell off in odd and even numbers* (always commencing on the right, in counting)—TELL OFF! *Form ranks*—MARCH!" (This order must hereafter take the place of the long one before used, viz.: "Odd numbers stand fast; even numbers, an oblique step to the right and rear—march!" Let this forming ranks be well done.) "*Ranks, right and left*—FACE! *Form company*—MARCH! *Right*—DRESS! FRONT! *Tell off in whole uumbers*—TELL OFF!" (We will suppose there are twenty-four: if there is an uneven number, consult note at the end of this drill.) "*Tell off in sections of six*—TELL OFF! *First section, stand fast; second, third, and fourth sections*—LEFT FACE! *Prove distance*—MARCH! (See previous drill.) FRONT! *Sections, Right*—DRESS! FRONT! *Non-commissioned officers*—(here the 2d sergeant commands, to his rear rank, "*Right*—FACE!") *to your posts*—MARCH!" (The 2d sergeant, followed by the other sergeants and corporals, marches up the rear of the line, [see dotted line in the plate,] turns square corners, marches down the line, and, as each officer comes opposite his place, he steps in, with a "right face," and halts in line. Each sergeant takes the right, and each corporal the left, of his section.) The orderly now commands, "*Sergeants, three paces to the front*—MARCH!" (These start with left foot, and keep time.) When they have done this, the orderly, following the dotted line in the plate, marches to "1^b," faces the company, and orders, "*Company*—SALUTE!" As soon as this is done, the orderly makes an "about face," marches a pace or two towards the captain, at "1^c," salutes him, (the captain returns it,) and then marches, by the dotted line, to his post, "1^d," makes an "about face," and comes into line with the other sergeants. He has now finished his duties, and the captain (or yourself) takes command, by saying, " *Officers, to your posts*—MARCH!" The sergeants come, simultaneously, to an "about face," march directly *into* line, facing the rear, make another "about face," and are at their posts. At the same time the lieutenants march to their posts, which are pointed out in the plate.

Note.—According to rule, the position of the 2d lieutenant is at the extreme left of the company; the place designated on the plate seems, on some accounts, to be the more convenient one.

It should be explained here, that if the company have arms, the order, instead of being " Company—Salute," should be " *Company—present* ARMS!" and they should remain "at a present," until the captain takes command and orders, " *Company—shoulder* ARMS!" Then follows, " *Officers, to your posts*—MARCH!"

This drill may well be wholly occupied in practising this "forming company." It is, when well done, a very pretty movement.

DRILL EIGHTH.

The orderly forms company. During a part of this drill, the sergeants and corporals are to drill as privates, but at their posts. The commissioned officers are to be observing your commands.

The "Rest at ease" consists in only this: the left foot must remain in line, while all the rest of the body takes recess. Talking is allowed, in a low tone; but no one may touch his neighbor, (except when accoutrements are in use, and it is necessary to have them adjusted.)

Give the whole company, "REST! ATTENTION! *Rest*—AT EASE!"

Now drill the 1st Section by itself, as follows: "*1st Section,*—ATTENTION! *Mark time*—MARCH! HALT!" (The command "Guide right," means that each man shall feel the elbow of his right-hand man, without crowding him, and, while marching, shall take care not to leave his side. "Guide left" is the converse of this. If these commands are obeyed, the line need not be broken.) "*Mark time*—MARCH! *Forward—three paces—guide right*—MARCH!" (The word "march" must be given just as the *right* foot touches the ground. They can then start off with the left. Take care that they march *only* three paces. They must count, mentally, "one, two, three," and halt. Give the same commands again.) "*1st Section, about*—FACE! *Mark time*—MARCH! *Forward*—MARCH!" (Now, to halt them in line, facing the rear, give the word, "Halt" on the step before the one which would bring them in.

Give them an "about face," when they will be in line.) "*Right*—DRESS! FRONT! *Rest*—AT EASE!"

Drill the other sections in the same exercises. Try to excite rivalry between the sections.

Return to the 1st Section. "*1st Section—right into line*—MARCH!"—See plate No. 3. The idea of the movement is that the whole section, which now faces *front*, in line, shall face *right*, in line. At the words, "Right into line," the sergeant of the section makes a "right face," and the rest make a *half* "right face," (See plate No. 1,) with their right shoulders then in line; each man faces that place which he is to occupy in the new position. At the word "march," each marches straight forward to that place; the man next to the sergeant takes one step, the next man two, and so on. Of course they must march in time, and perhaps it will be necessary to require marking time, before giving the order. Say to them that they "must dress as they come into line" with the sergeant.

In this and the following movements, you had better copy the plates on a large sheet of paper, and explain the movement to each member of the section.

To return to former position, the command is, "*First section, right*—FACE! *Left into line*—MARCH!" (See plate No. 3.) At the words, "Left into line," the sergeant comes to an "about," and the rest make a *half* "right face," (See plate No. 1,) their *left* shoulders thrown forward; at the word "march!" the sergeant completes the "about face," and is at his original post, and the rest march towards a point a little to the *right* of their old places in line, take one step *beyond* the line, turn to the right, and come into line at their original positions.

Both of these movements are difficult, the most difficult your troops have had, especially the last. To insure success, be sure that you yourself know just what is to be done, and then endeavor to give them as clear ideas of it as possible, by means of diagrams, or by marking lines on the ground, or chalking them on a floor. It is necessary that these be thoroughly learned, because they form parts of movements to be learned hereafter.

Drill each section separately on these. When they have each learned them, let them all do them together. Here your sergeants have something to do. Your command is, "*Sections—right into line*—(at this, each sergeant stept briskly to the front of his section, and orders, "*first* [or other] *section*—RIGHT *into line;* the sections are not to move at *your* command, but at that of their sergeants)—MARCH!" When the movement is completed, each sergeant orders, "*first* (or other) *section—left dress!*" and takes his position in front of his section, two paces in front of it, and facing the captain.

While performing this movement, the corporals have something to do. It is the duty of the second corporal to take position directly in the rear of the first corporal, and of the third and fourth corporals to stand directly in the rear of the others. This keeps "the column" straight. Each sergeant gives "Left dress" instead of "Right dress," because the sections must dress by the corporals, who are on the left.

The company is now "in column of sections to the front." It is in marching order, and the position of the officers are shown in the plate, No. 4.

To return into line, the captain commands, "*Company—right*, FACE! *Sections, left into line*—(Here each sergeant turns to his section, and orders, '*first* [or other] *section*, LEFT *into line!*' and then takes his own position at the right of his section, facing right, but at the first position of an 'about face,' doing all this *very* briskly,)—MARCH!" (Here each sergeant and his section executes the movement as taught above.)

The company is now "in line" again. This will be a long drill, and some Saturday afternoon will be a good time to devote to it. There must be considerable repetition and a great deal of patience, on the part of both teacher and learners. But the movements are worth learning well, for they are brilliant and "showy."

DRILL NINTH.

We have now accomplished quite an amount in the way of drill and discipline. On some accounts I should prefer to continue drilling without arms, but, for variety, and to satisfy the boys, who have all this time been longing for guns, we will introduce them.

I shall suppose that you are provided with real guns, or at least with something resembling them, for you may have guns; if you have lances, you can easily adapt these instructions to that innocent weapon.

At the command, "Fall in!" each private and corporal takes his gun (they are supposed to be numbered, in a rack), and takes his place in line. At the word, "Attention," the butt of his gun should rest on the ground (the trigger side out), about three inches from his right foot, and on a line with the toes. The right arm should form a right angle at the elbow, and the hand grasp the barrel of the gun. In order that the gun shall not be placed too far forward, the elbow should be drawn back, so that the barrel shall almost rest against the shoulder; at any rate, so that the piece shall stand as nearly perpendicular as possible. In other respects, "the position of the soldier" should be preserved.

"Shoulder arms" is done in three motions. First: the right hand, keeping its grasp, raises the piece perpendicularly against the right shoulder, and, at the same time, the left hand is thrown briskly across the breast, and grasps the piece just below the right hand. Second: the right hand comes down briskly, and grasps the piece at the lock. Third: the left hand is brought back to its side. These motions must be executed by all in exactly the same time. Take care that the body is not swayed about by the motion of the arms. "Remember the *poker!*"

The grasp by right hand at the lock is, the first finger below the "trigger-guard," the thumb above it, and the other fingers around the hammer; the weight being thus sustained by the projections, viz., the hammer and the trigger-guard.

Until facility is acquired in executing this command, the order should be, "*Shoulder arms in three motions*—ONE—TWO—THREE!" Let each motion be done with so much muscular energy that it may be heard by all. "Make the motion *tell!*"

"*Order arms in three motions*—ONE—TWO—THREE!" This is exactly the reverse of "shoulder arms." 1st. The left hand is brought across the breast and grasps the barrel, where it did before. 2d. The right hand is raised, and grasps the piece above the left hand. 3d. The left hand is returned to its side, and, at the same instant, the right hand allows the piece to come briskly to the ground, at the position of "Attention."

Try these commands alternately. You cannot ex

pect perfection in this drill, but you must get as near it as you can.

After much practice, you may try these movements without counting the motions. The orders will be simply, "*Shoulder*—ARMS!" and "*Order*—ARMS!" *They* must count, however, remembering the time you gave them. I should have said that the time given for the "one, two, three," should be, at first, in seconds, or even more slowly. You may shorten the intervals as fast as they acquire skill.

These two exercises in the "manual of arms" will be enough for one time. The drill may be diversified by a review of the first three drills, and anything else already practised.

At this drill it will be necessary to omit "the salute;" their right hands are occupied. They will soon learn the "Present arms," which will take the place of the salute.

REMARKS.

Your orderly is bound to report absences, and *all* officers to report misdemeanors. Teach your boys to discriminate between the "reports" of an officer desirous of doing his duty, and of a companion who tells only as a "tell-tale."

You must use your own judgment in regard to government, remembering, however, that you are "major" of the company, the highest in command, and as such, an autocrat in the strictest sense of the term.

Now that you are so well advanced it will be well to have music. (Consult chapter on "Uniform, &c.") It is *better* to drill mostly without music. The boys will easily acquire a kind of rhythmic instinct in marching, which is better for them than *dependence* on the tap of the drum. But boys are anxious to hear the music of a drum and fife, and it is well to gratify them.

Your music, on the drill-ground, must occupy a particular position, never leaving it except when the *company* is marching. The musicians are to listen to your commands *and be ready always to strike the drum promptly at the word "march."* In all brief movements, such as "Right or left into line—march!" a mere tap of the drum is sufficient; and this, perhaps, is unnecessary.

I may as well say here, and might have done so before, that it is *impossible* for me to speak of *everything* connected with this complicated matter of military discipline. Much, very much, must be left to your judgment and discretion.

I should add, also, that, in some respects, my instructions are not strictly in accordance with United States army rules. When I differ, it is either because I have purposely modified certain rules to adapt them to boys, or because I forget them. These latter changes or errors will, I hope, be few, and I am sure they will be unimportant.

DRILL TENTH.

Fall in, in line, without sizing or forming sections. We will practise the "Present arms," and then form company regularly.

Review "Shoulder arms" and "Order arms."

"Present arms" is done from "a shoulder," in two motions. At "one," the right hand raises the piece so high that the hand is against the thigh: at the same time the left arm is thrown across the breast horizontally, and grasps the barrel, and the right hand, taking advantage of the support given the gun by the left hand, changes its grasp in such manner that the piece may not be turned around when it shall be brought forward; at "two" the piece is brought briskly up, the rammer outwards, and is held directly in front of the nose. The left hand grasps the barrel stiffly, the arm, at the elbow, being pressed to the side and forming an exact right angle; the fingers grasp the barrel and the thumb is erect against the side of it. To make the right angle, the left hand must be lowered, slipped down the stock, after the gun is in position. The grasp of the right hand is at the small, round part of the stock, below the lock, all the fingers in front.

Great care must be taken that these directions are all *strictly* observed; for, if they are not, the guns will not be held perpendicularly; they will be uneven in height, and held either too near, or too far from the body. All these are to be guarded against.

"Shoulder arms," "from a Present," is the reverse of "Present arms." At one motion the piece is brought back to the side, the right hand resuming the grasp used in "Shoulder arms," and the left held against it with the fingers flat, not grasping it, merely to steady the gun against the shoulder: at the second motion, the left hand is brought back promptly to its side.

In both of these two new exercises the commands must be, at first, "*Present arms in two motions*—ONE—TWO!" "*Shoulder arms in two motions*—ONE—TWO!" Time, seconds.

I beg the drill master to believe me that, in these instructions, I use *no waste words.* He will need, for success, to take care that they are obeyed *in every particular.*

Company may now be formed in the usual way. At the place where the orderly has commanded "Salute," he may now order "Present arms," and they are to remain "at a Present" until the orderly has gone to his post in a line with the other sergeants, when the captain commands, "*Company—shoulder* ARMS! followed by, "*Officers to your posts*—MARCH!"

Note.—At the "present arms," when company is formed, the drums should beat a triple roll, two sounds to a roll.

"Support arms" is done in one motion, "from a shoulder." The right hand, without altering its grasp, brings the piece obliquely across the body; the barrel still rests at the right shoulder, but the stock rests at the middle of the abdomen, and the left hand is laid across the right. If the gun is pressed too tightly against the abdomen, the barrel will stand out from the shoulder, which is to be avoided.

"Carry arms" "from a support," is merely bringing the piece back to the position of "Shoulder arms," and returning the left hand to its side. These motions must be done together, and *all* motions done PROMPTLY.

In the position of "Shoulder arms," the right arm must be extended to its full length, not at all crooked at the elbow; the barrel must rest in the hollow of the right shoulder, and the stock be pressed against the side of the leg.

In movements, the guns should be carried at "Shoulder arms," but "Support arms" must be frequently given for a change.

Review as much as possible in this drill, consistently with learning these new items from the manual.

Hereafter dismiss company at a "Right face," in file.

DRILL ELEVENTH.

Review the manual of arms in the following order: *Shoulder*—ARMS! *Order*—ARMS! *Shoulder*—ARMS! *Support*—ARMS! *Carry*—ARMS! *Present*—ARMS! *Shoulder*—ARMS! *Order*—ARMS! REST!

"REST," under arms, differs but little from "Rest" heretofore learned. The position of the feet is the same, (see plate No. 1.) As this position is assumed, the gun ("at an order") leans back on the shoulder, the right hand lets go its grasp and is brought across the abdomen, where it is crossed by the left hand: the piece then rests on the ground, in the hollow of the right arm and against the shoulder.

"Attention," from "Rest," differs but little from the same command before learned. The gun is grasped by the right hand, the butt placed on a line with the toes, the feet brought to the V position, and the left hand carried back to its side: all these done at the same instant.

Remember that no movements can be made while the guns are on the ground.

"From a rest," the new commands of this drill are: "*Company*—ATTENTION! *Shoulder*—ARMS! *Centre*—FACE!" (See plate No. 5.) At this, the corporal of the 2d section, and the sergeant of the 3d section, take one step forward, elbow to elbow: the 1st and

2d sections (or, as they should be called, "the 1st Platoon") face *left*, towards the centre; the 2d Platoon (3d and 4th sections) face *right*, towards the centre. The corporal and sergeant above-mentioned, are now to be the file leaders of the company, in double file; they march (at the words "*Forward*—MARCH!") straight ahead, and the next two behind them march up to each other, face to face, turn, one to the right and the other to the left, touch elbows and follow, "at a fronting distance," their file leaders: the others do the same. The lieutenants fall in and close up the file.

The file leaders must be instructed to march forward in a perfectly straight line, aiming at some particular point: the men behind them must march as in single file, but each two keeping exactly together.

To turn to the right or left, "File right," or, "File left," is given. Suppose the latter; then the sergeant, who is on the left, turns in his tracks, the corporal wheeling around him as a pivot, taking care not to leave his side. Here an exact right angle is made, and as each couple comes up to the angle, they turn in the same way. "*Make a square corner.*"

When the company is marched out so that all are clear of any turning point, the captain halts in front of the file leaders and commands, "*Into line*—MARCH!" (See plate No. 5.) The file leaders halt: the rest march up directly behind them, turn, the left-hand man to the left, and the right-hand man to the right; each marches along the rear of the line which is forming, and steps into his place, dressing, as he comes into line, by the two file leaders.

The company is now "in line," as at first. They will need a "Right dress." Try this over again, this time marching longer in double file.

In marching, the taller boys will naturally take longer steps than the short ones. To remedy this, urge that the first take shorter steps than they are naturally inclined to, and the latter longer. While marching, advise, "If you find yourselves falling behind your file leaders, gain on them, not by hurrying the time, (taking *faster* steps,) but by increasing the pace, (taking *longer* steps.) Always keep at a 'fronting distance' from them."

Bring them into line again. Take care, *always*, to turn at right angles. Let the rear files march fully up to the rear of the line before turning. Let them march along the rear so closely as to almost touch the coat tails of the line, and come squarely into place.

The captain will, during these movements, occasionally command, "*Company, support* (or *carry*)—ARMS!" This is done for the relief of change. But it may be observed that "Support arms" is most convenient when the men are "in file," single or double; and that "Carry arms" is best when "in line."

After a rest "in line," practice the following new exercise from the manual.

"Trail arms," "from a shoulder," is done in three motions. At "one," let the gun fall forward from the shoulder into the palm and grasp of the left hand, which is to be thrown there to receive it; at "two," let the left hand support the piece, while the right hand changes grasp, and catches the gun at that point where it will balance itself in the hand: at "Three," let the left hand return to its side, and, at the same instant, the right arm drop its full length, carrying the gun in such a manner that the bayonet (if there is one) is on a level with the eye. Each of these motions must be made *distinctly*, so that it may be heard all along the line. Instructor commands,—"*Trail arms in three motions*, ONE, TWO, THREE!" and counts in seconds.

When this is learned tolerably well, practice it without counting.

Review the whole manual now learned.

Review "Right (and left) into line," by sections, and then by company. Take care that the sergeants give their commands briskly and distinctly.

If time allows, review other movements, especially "the facings."

DRILL TWELFTH.

After forming company, drill in marching three (or more) paces forward, with a "guide right;" do this first by single sections, next by platoons, and lastly, by "front of company." To march "by front of company" a given number of paces (or until the word "halt") without breaking the line, so that, at the halt, no one is either too far in front or rear, and so that there shall be no need of "dressing the line" after the halt,—this is an achievement to be proud of. To do it well, the importance of the "guide right or left" must be insisted on; in this, let there be no actual *pressing* towards the right or left, but let the elbows be in close and constant contact. Let the length of pace be thought of; and the *difference* in pace between the taller and shorter boys. The latter are at the centre of the line, the former at the wings; and if great care be not taken, the line will become crescent-shaped, the centre being behind. Execute this *well*, and you will receive praise from military critics.

Change the programme of drill by introducing practice in the manual.

"*Charge*—BAYONET!" This is done, "from a shoulder," in one motion. At the last word, the feet assume "the first position of an about face," the left knee is bent, and the body leaned slightly forward; at the same time the piece is allowed to fall briskly into the left hand, as in "Trail arms," and is firmly grasped by both hands and held by both, with the bayonet on a level with the eye. "Every eye to the front!" Here (and the remark applies also to "Trail arms") the pieces should all be in line, that is, should have the same inclination. If they are at different inclinations, order "*Dress your pieces by the right!*" that is, let all have the same inclination as that of the piece of the right-hand man. "Be BRISK, boys!"

"Shoulder arms" brings us back to the original position.

Practise this a long time. It is a very "showy" movement.

"*Centre*—FACE! *Forward*—MARCH! *Outward countermarch*—MARCH!" (See plate No. 6.) At this the captain stands at the head of the advancing column and the files separate as they come up to him, the right-hand file turns to the right, the other file to the left, and they march in a direction opposite to that which they were pursuing. They march as far as is convenient, and at the command, "*Inward countermarch*—MARCH!" the two file-leaders face about, come together elbow to elbow, and march in the original direction, the others imitating them as fast as they come up to the position just left by the file-leaders.

During the "outward countermarch," care must be taken that the file leaders march on a line with each other, and that their followers also are exactly opposite each other.

In these drills, let the teacher take care that the "first principles," as taught in our earlier drills, are not forgotten. If at all necessary, let a whole drill—say a Saturday afternoon—be devoted to a general-review. Insist, constantly, on the preservation of "the position of the soldier." Let the duty of watching for and correcting the evils of laxity in these "first principles, be assigned to all the officers, especially to the two lieutenants. Your captain must be mainly engaged in observing the commands you give, and their execution.

DRILL THIRTEENTH.

"*Outward countermarch by two's*—MARCH!" (See plate No. 6.) This is done while marching in double file. as from "Centre face." At the last word, the leader of each file turns to march in an opposite direction, as in the previous drill: he steps a little further out, and the second in file turns and marches at his side, being the inner man. Numbers three and four, five and six, and so on, of each file, do the same at the turning point. The result is, that as the outward countermarchers advance, (their backs to the captain,) they go "by two's."

"*Inward countermarch*—MARCH!" At this,—given when all have passed the turning point, and the two first couples are in a line with each other,—these wheel inward, the two inner men acting as pivots, and the two outer men come elbow to elbow; the four now form a line and march toward the captain. If the first command is repeated, the four again separate into the original two's, and the movement is repeated. If the captain wishes them to resume the plain double file movement, as at first, he orders, "*By double file—forward*, MARCH!"

"*Outward countermarch by four's*—MARCH!" (see plate No. 7,) is a duplication of countermarching by two's. The first four of each file turn outward together, the first man stepping still further out, and the second, third, and fourth forming in line with him.

"Inward countermarch by four's," is best explained by the diagram. At the word "march," the two inner men act as pivots, around whom the others wheel; the two outer men join elbows, and lines of eight march towards the captain.

As either of the last combinations (by two's and four's) return toward the captain, he may command:

"*Outward countermarch in single file*—MARCH!" (See plate.) At this, each man remembers his number, whether first or second, or first, second, third or fourth, and forms in single file accordingly.

Countermarching is always an effective and attractive movement, when well done. Practise it very thoroughly and carefully.

On parade, or at other times, it may be necessary or advisable to "ground arms." This is done, "from an order," in two motions:—at "One," the pieces are turned sidewise, so that the locks are nearest the leg; at "Two," the left foot takes a long pace forward, and the body is leaned forward so that the right hand may deposit the piece on the ground. The right foot does not leave its place in line. It is hardly necessary to practise this by motions. Tell them to turn the piece at the word "ground," and to do the remainder at the last word.

"*Take*—ARMS!" is the reverse of "Ground arms;" there needs no other explanation.

When arms are "grounded" on parade, and the company takes recess, a guard must always be placed over the guns. The guard may consist of one, but two are better. If the recess is a long one, the guard must be relieved once or twice. The orderly sergeant appoints and instructs the guard. He may choose them in alphabetical order, or in any other way. After the company is dismissed, the orderly commands: "*Guards*—ATTENTION! *Shoulder*—ARMS! (They stand side by side.) *To your posts*—MARCH!" One takes the extreme right, the other the left, of the line of guns; they face each other, and at the word "MARCH," they advance toward each other; they meet half-way, halt, present arms (face to face), shoulder arms, about face, and return. As they come to the end of their beat, they are not to turn carelessly, but to halt, about face, and then return to the half-way point. They are particularly observed, because they are individualized, and the honor of the company rests on them.

When coming to an "about face" under arms, the left

hand is to be thrown across the piece ("at a shoulder,") to steady it while turning.

I prefer to introduce but one or two novelties into each of the drills at this time, because there is *so much to be done in reviewing.*

DRILL FOURTEENTH.

To form front of company by platoons, from sections, (See plate No. 8,) the captain will command: "*Company, by platoons, forward*—MARCH!" (If the company is already marching, the word "forward" is to be omitted.) At the command "March," the 1st and 3d sergeants will command, "1*st* (or 3*d*) *Section, by the right flank, file right*—MARCH!" They will march in that direction until the right of the 2d (or 4th) section joins the left of the 1st (or 3d), when the sergeants will command, "FRONT!" and then the two sections will march forward together in line, as a platoon.

To return into sections, the command is, "*Company, by sections, forward*—MARCH!" Then the 1st and 3d sections march right on; but the sergeants of the 2d and 4th sections command, "2*d* (or 4*th*) *Section, by the right flank, file right*—MARCH!" He marches them in that direction until they are again in the rear of the 1st or 3d sections, (the corporals being guides,) when they command, "FRONT!" and then all march as sections again.

If, during the execution of these movements, the sections are not in line, the sergeants must order a "guide left." If the platoons are broken in line, it is the duty of the lieutenants to order the "guide left."

But, while marching by platoons, the command may be given, "*By front of company*—MARCH!" when the same movement above explained for sections may be executed by platoons. The 1st platoon, at command of the 1st lieutenant, marches by file right, and fronts just as the right of the 2d platoon reaches and joins its left.

At any time while marching, whether by front of company, or by platoons or sections, all may be brought into single file by the following command: (we will suppose that the company is marching in sections,) "*Sections, by the right flank, file left*—MARCH!" At the words "right flank, file left," each sergeant goes to the right of his section; he marches forward in the direction in which all were marching before, but the rest of the section, at the word "march," faces right, files left and follows the sergeant; he marches on (for instance, the 2d sergeant,) and comes behind the corporal of the section (for instance, the 1st,) in front of him; and thus all are in file. The same principle applies to platoons, the lieutenants taking the duties of the sergeants when the movement is done in sections.

I give no illustration of these movements, because my instructions are, I think, explicit, and because I wish the drill master to *think them out*, and make his own diagrams.

A good use of this movement may be made as follows:—Suppose your company is marching in a muddy street, and you wish to get on the sidewalk; as your 1st section comes up to the cross-walk, command, "*Sections, by the right (or left) flank, file right*, (or if left, the corporals are file leaders; sergeants on the right) MARCH!" As soon as the sergeant reaches the middle of the sidewalk, order a "file right" or "file left."

Draw lines on the ground for imaginary sidewalks, explain to your men the object of the movement, and practise it, both to the right and left.

Now, to come from single file into sections, as, for instance, from the right-hand sidewalk into the street, command, "*Company, form column of sections to the front*—MARCH!" The 1st sergeant commands, at the word "front," "*1st section, file left*," and as soon as the whole section is on the cross-walk, he commands, "*Front!*" The other sections, as they come up to the place just vacated by the 1st section, imitate its movements, each sergeant taking care to command, "Front," just when he sees his corporal on a line with the one in advance.

Plate No. 8, gives other examples of forming sections from single file. Study it carefully.

In these directions, and, I suppose, in many others,

there may seem to be much that is inexplicitly and confusedly expressed. I doubt whether it is possible to make these movements intelligible at a glance; but I believe that if the teacher will give as careful a study to this treatise as he would to the works of a Latin or Greek author, he will not fail to understand it.

In marching in the street, obstructions are sometimes met. The company will probably be marching by sections, the usual way. If it is desired that the company march from the middle to the side of the street, (say the right,) command, "*Company, by the right flank, file* RIGHT!" When they are sufficiently near the side, order "FRONT!" At the first command, each section faces to the right, and in distinct and independent file, marches in that direction. "Front" brings them into the original direction. But they are now, after having passed the obstruction, too far on one side of the street; "*Company, by the left flank, file* LEFT! FRONT!" brings them back.

DRILL FIFTEENTH.

In this drill I shall endeavor to present a *series* of movements, which may possibly serve the captain as a programme for parade. I shall explain only the new movements.

It will be an excellent lesson for the "major" or captain to draw off, on paper or the black-board, a diagram of the whole, in connection.

Company is at rest, in line.

"*Company*—ATTENTION! *Right*—FACE! *Sections, right into line*—(each sergeant repeats the command, standing in front of, and applying it to his section,)—MARCH! *Company, forward*, MARCH! *Sections, by the right flank, file right*—MARCH! *Company*, FRONT! (Sergeants must attend to their sections, and order a "guide left," if necessary.) *Sections, by the left turn*—MARCH!" (See plate, No. 9.) At the word "turn," the 1st lieutenant (or "1st guide;" see paragraph at end of this drill) takes position beside the corporal of the 1st section, standing there to mark the turning spot for the other sections; and at the same word, the 1st sergeant commands, "*1st section, by the left turn.*" At the word, "March," from the captain, the section turns, as shown in the plate. In turning, the line must not be broken, and a "guide left" may be necessary from the sergeants. As the 2d section approaches the turning point, the 2d sergeant commands, "*2d section, by the left turn*," and as soon as his corporal touches the point opposite the lieutenant, he adds, "MARCH!" The 2d lieutenant has now reached the turning point, and he assumes the place of guide, while the 1st lieutenant advances to his post. The 3d and 4th sergeants and sections imitate the example of the 2d. As soon as the 4th section has turned, the 2d lieutenant takes long steps and regains his post.

"*Company, by platoons,* MARCH! *Platoons, by the left turn,*—(the lieutenants command their platoons as the sergeants did their sections)—MARCH! *Company, by front of company,*—MARCH! HALT! (until this word the company had been constantly in motion.) *Right*—DRESS! *Support*—ARMS! *To the rear, centre*—FACE! ('To the rear,' is something new. At the word, 'rear' the two file leaders,—who, in 'Centre—face' have taken a step together in advance,—come to the first position of an about 'face,' and at the word 'face,' they about face.) *Forward*—MARCH! *File*—RIGHT! *File*—LEFT! *Outward countermarch in single file*—MARCH! *Inward countermarch*—MARCH! *Outward countermarch by two's*—MARCH! *Inward countermarch*—MARCH! *Outward countermarch by four's*—MARCH! *Inward countermarch*—MARCH! *Outward countermarch by sections in circle*—MARCH. (At the word 'march,' each section marches in a circle [See plate No. 10.] They revolve several times, and then, as the captain sees that the two file leaders are coming together, he commands, '*Forward*—MARCH!') *Outward countermarch in circles by platoons*—MARCH. (The principle is the same as 'in circles by sections.') *Forward*—MARCH! *Into line*—MARCH! *Right*—DRESS!"

"Front," after a "right" or "left dress," has been

omitted, and will be, because it has been remarked that that command *always* follows a "dress."

Practise now the manual of arms. The *order* of this manual may be varied; but the captain must have discovered that there are certain commands which cannot follow each other; for instance, "Order arms" cannot follow a "Present arms," and *vice versa.*

Note.—"Guides" are an addition to a company, but are not necessary; for, as has been seen, the lieutenants may do their duties. However, it is really beneath the dignity of a commissioned officer to do such duty. "The guides" may be the two smallest boys in the company. They may carry lances, with small streamers, painted (gilt on blue), with the name of the company. Their posts are, while marching, at the rear of the 4th section, one in the rear of the sergeant and the other of the corporal, two paces off. When "in line," their posts are at the extremes. When the line is to advance by front, to a new alignment (new position of line), they may be stationed as points to march to. A command in such a case, would be, "*Company, forward, guide right, to the alignment of the guides*—MARCH!" They are also to stand at all turning points, the 1st guide being relieved by the 2d as soon as half the company has passed the point.

DRILL SIXTEENTH.

While in sections, marching or not marching, the command may be given, "*To the left, arms' length*—EXTEND! At the last word, each man, except the corporal, extends his left arm, and places his left hand on the right shoulder of his neighbor, at the same time all taking a side step, in time (a left-oblique step, if marching), until they are at such a distance from each other that only the fingers of the hands rest on the shoulders. At the command, "*Arms*—DOWN!" each arm returns, promptly, to its side.

This movement makes a fine display of the company.

While marching thus, in open order, each man must take care to march exactly in the rear of the man in front of him in the section in front; and he must also take care not to break the line of his own section.

"*To the right close*—MARCH!" brings them back. All except the right-hand man take a side step, in time, to the right (if marching, an oblique step), until elbows touch.

"*Company form cross on 2d section*—MARCH!" (See plate No. 11.) The company is in line. 2d sergeant commands, "*2d section, stand*—FAST! 1st sergeant commands, "*1st section, one pace forward*—MARCH! *Left turn*—MARCH!" and he marches his section to its position, as shown in the plate. 3d sergeant commands, "3*d section, right*—FACE! *File right*—MARCH! FRONT!" The "front" of this section is shown in the plate. 4th sergeant commands, "*4th section, right*—FACE! *On right by file into line*—MARCH!

"On right by file into line," is a new movement. (See plate No. 9.) The section is at a "Right face;" at the word "March," the right-hand man faces right, and takes one step forward, and the section, in file, marches behind him, the second man coming beside him as soon as he passes his back, the third man passes on by the second, and comes beside him, and so on.

The sections are now in the form of a cross, with the corporals at the centre. Observe in the diagram, in which direction each section faces. (See plate No. 11.)

While in this form, command, "*Sections, left turn, guide left*—MARCH! Sergeants seek the right of their sections, move with them, and in an under tone, insist on the "guide left." Let the right angles of the cross be exactly preserved. Turn once or twice completely around, back to place.

Another movement in form of a cross results from the commands, from the captain, "2*d section, right*—FACE! 1*st section, about*—FACE! 4*th section, left*—FACE! (All are now facing in the same direction.) *Company, forward*—MARCH!" Let them march a few yards in this direction, the lieutenant taking care that the form of the cross is preserved, and thus command, "*By the right flank*—MARCH!" At the last word, all turn, briskly, to the right, and continue marching as they face. "*By the left flank*—MARCH!" is similar to the previous command. By means of a "halt," and an "about face," they may be made to march in still another direction.

There are two ways by which the line, or front of company may be reässumed from a cross. (The sections must first be faced as in the diagram.)

The first is by reversing the process of formation. Command, "*Company, reduce cross and form front of company on 2d Section*—MARCH!" Sergeants command: "*2d Section, stand*—FAST. *1st Section, about*—FACE! *Forward*—MARCH! (Until the left rests on the right of 2d section.) *Right*—TURN! (They are now in line, facing to the rear.) *About*—FACE! *4th Section, right*—FACE! *Left, by file into line*—MARCH! (This is done in a manner exactly the reverse of that by which they were formed in cross.) *3d Section, left*—FACE! *File left*—MARCH!"

All are now in line. Give a "right dress."

The second method introduces a novelty, and the movement is more easily, rapidly, and showily executed. (See plate No. 12.)

Command, "*Sections, form circle*—MARCH!" At the word "circle," each sergeant goes to the right of his section, and commands a "right face," and himself files left, and at the word "march" he leads his file into a circle, as shown in the diagram. The circle must be complete, that is, without gaps between the ends of sections. The commissioned officers must have contrived to stand in the centre of the circle.

After marching once or twice around, the captain may command, "*Company, by file, forward*—MARCH!" whereupon the orderly sergeant marches straight forward, (leaving the circle,) followed by the rest, in file. The circle is now straightened out, and the company is marching in file. "*Company*—HALT!" The captain, standing on the left of the advancing file, commands, "FRONT!" and the company is once more "in line."

In marching "by the right flank," that is, from a "right face" or "file right," "Front" is executed by facing to the left; "by the left flank," by facing to the right.

The maneuvres of forming cross, and the various movements while in that form, are, perhaps, the most showy of any that can be executed. They should be *perfectly* learned.

DRILL SEVENTEENTH.

The company is in line.

"*Company, form square on second section,*—MARCH!" (See plate No. 14.) Sergeants command :—"*2d Section, stand* FAST! *1st Section, about* FACE! *Right*—TURN! (They turn until they make a right angle with the 2d section.) HALT! *About*—FACE!

"3d *Section, Right*—FACE! *File right*—MARCH! (They turn until the left of this section reaches the left of the second.) HALT! *Left*—FACE! *Right*—TURN! They turn until this section makes a right angle with the 1st section.) HALT!

"4th *Section, Right*—FACE. *Forward*—MARCH! (They march until this section reaches the left of 2d section). HALT! *Right*—FACE! *Left*—TURN! (They turn until this section comes to its place in the square.) HALT! *About*—FACE!"

The square is now formed, all facing outwards. Commissioned officers should be in the centre of the square. Care should be taken that the angles are all right angles, and that the sides are "dressed."

By so commanding that all shall face in the same direction, there may be marching in the form of a square, as was done in the form of a cross.

To return into line, reverse the process of formation. The instructor ought, by this time, to be able to do this without explanations.

While in form of square, practise the manual of arms.

An effective movement while in square results from the commands, "*Company, charge*—BAYONET! *Sections five* (or more) *paces forward*—MARCH! *Shoulder*—ARMS! *About*—FACE! *Into square*—MARCH!" At the last word, they march back to the lines of the square, halt and about face, without commands for these movements.

Company in line. "*Right*—FACE! *File*—RIGHT! (again), *File*—RIGHT! *Right by file into line, two paces distant*—MARCH!" (See plate No. 15.) The execution of this differs from that in the movements of a single section, as before taught, only in this, that it is done by the whole company and that, instead of forming in close order, each man passes two paces beyond the last in line and then steps squarely into line. If there is not room for the whole line in any one direction, order, "Break ground to the right, or left."

To return to a close line, command, "*Company, right* FACE! *In close order, into line*, MARCH!" The file leader (orderly) retains his position; the rest march on, not increasing or lessening their distances between them, until they reach their file leader in line, when they turn squarely into line.

DRILL EIGHTEENTH.

In this chapter will be found various exercises and movements, together with general information, some or all of which may be introduced into this drill.

The "oblique step" is often useful, in cases of meeting obstructions of any kind, or in closing ranks after "an extend."

"*Right oblique*—MARCH!" (See plate No. 16.) If from a halt, carry the right foot obliquely to the right and front about twenty-two inches from the left foot, and sixteen toward that side; carry the left foot sixteen inches in front of the right heel. Take special care not to derange the head and shoulders,—that is, *keep them to the front*, and not in the oblique direction.

"Left oblique" is executed on the same principles.

"*Forward*—MARCH" brings all to the direct march.

"*Arms at* WILL!" It is necessary to give this command occasionally, during long marches on parade, and, sometimes, at drills.

At the command, the guns may be carried over the right shoulder, "at will." On long marches, "Trail arms" will be found a convenient way of carrying the guns; and at the command, "*Change*—TRAIL!" the gun may be shifted and carried by the left hand.

Sometimes the line may be located a few inches in advance or behind a desired line. To bring it forward, station the right-hand man at the end of the desired line and command, "*By file, right*—DRESS!" (or the left-hand man may be so stationed and "left dress" ordered.) At the word "dress," the second man, followed, one by one, by the others, will step forward and dress himself by the guide. The same movement may be executed backwards.

In marching by platoons or sections, if any such division has gained ground, that is, is too near the division in advance, command, for instance, "*2d Section, mark*—TIME!" At the last word, they will stop and, as it were, march in their tracks, until their proper position is attained, when "*Forward*—MARCH," will start them on again.

I omit giving "Fix and unfix bayonets," together with the manual of loading and firing, because I shall, hereafter, urgently advise the use of lances. If, however, guns are used, instructions on these points,—and on others which may seem desirable to be adopted by the instructor,—may be found in "Scott's Tactics," "Hardies' Rifle Tactics," "The Recruit," and other military works.

It may be discovered, by reference to these books, that the writer has not strictly adhered to "authority," but his reasons for deviating are that "authority" for *men* is not "authority" for boys, and, that instructions for men who are to be soldiers by profession, are not adapted for boys, who are only amateur soldiers.

The length of pace in marching, for boys, should be about twenty inches, on an average. Paces may be marked, on the ground or floor, of this length and all taught to acquire this step.

In a "turn," from a halt, the pivot man turns in his tracks. In turning, while marching, the pivot man should advance not more than seven or eight inches, while the outside man takes the full pace, and no more.

The swiftness of pace, in common time, should be at the rate of ninety steps in a minute.

As recruits enter the company, the sergeants, under the supervision of the major or captain, should instruct them in "first principles." They should be introduced into the company as soon as possible.

The position of the "color-bearer," while marching, is with the 3d sergeant, in sections, or in file: with the 2d lieutenant, while marching in platoons; at the centre of a cross; and inside of a square. While the company is executing other division or company movements, or the manual of arms, the color should be posted out of the way, and the bearer is not on other duty. The color-bearer is, by right, an ensign and a commissioned officer, but it may not seem advisable to give him any rank.

Promotions, resulting from vacancies or removals, should be from corporals to sergeants, and from sergeants to lieutenants. In the absence of a corporal, a private may be appointed in his place, *pro tem.;* in the absence of a sergeant, a lieutenant should fill the vacancy.

DRILL NINETEENTH.

The sword exercise of the sergeants is as follows:

"*Shoulder*—(or carry)—ARMS!" The gripe in the right hand, the arm extended, close at the side, the back of the blade resting in the hollow of the right shoulder.

"*Support*—ARMS!" The left arm forms an acute

angle at the elbow, and the blade rests, the edge outwards, in the left hand, the fingers uppermost.

"*Order*—ARMS!" or, "REST!" The sword is brought to rest with its point on the ground, on a line with the toes, and as far from them as the extended arm and length of blade will allow; the back of the hand outwards.

"*Present*—ARMS!" This is done in two motions. At the first, the sword is raised so that the hand rest on the upper buttons on the coat, the flat of the blade outward and the blade inclined forward: at the second, the sword is brought down as in "order arms," but the point does not touch the ground, and the palm of the hand is outward. These motions should be executed in time with the motions of the guns.

"*Trail*—ARMS!" The same position as in "shoulder arms!"

"*Charge*—BAYONET!" The sergeant takes a position with his feet precisely as do the privates; the sword is raised and held, horizontally, on a level with the eyes, the edge outwards.

The captain and lieutenants may carry their swords either "at a shoulder" or "a support."

The sergeants should be thoroughly drilled, in a separate division, in these exercises, and should never fail to execute the required movement, when commanded, on drill with the company or on parade.

DRILL TWENTIETH.

At a drill preparatory to a parade, practise everything which is intended to be displayed. If excellence has not been attained in any particular exercise, it is better to omit it on parade ; sufficient variety may be given even if several movements are omitted. Besides, it is best to reserve some maneuvres for future parades.

Endeavor to infuse into the minds of all a spirit of determination to do the best possible.

Take care that the sergeants remember and understand their commands, positions and general duties.

At your first parade, it may be contrived that your colors shall be presented, by ladies, perhaps. Receive them in line, sergeants three paces to the front, lieutenants, five paces, captain, seven ; let *all* "present arms." This same salute may be given to individuals, for instance, to a person who has addressed the company ; or it may be given at the houses (to the families) of officers of the company, or distinguished persons.

Let a programme be carefully prepared of the streets to be passed through, and, particularly, of the movements to be made. Unless this is done, the commanding officer may become confused, and make mistakes.

Your captain may, or may not, be entrusted with

the sole command. If he is to be, he should have had frequent opportunities to practise commanding, and, especially, should have entire command at this preparatory drill. If the teacher commands, it is in the rank of "major," and he should march with the captain, to whom he should entrust some commands, and as many as possible.

I would advise, as a programme for parade, the following movements, the company being in line, and at rest:—

ATTENTION!
Shoulder—ARMS!
Right—FACE!
Left—FACE!
About—FACE!
About—FACE!
Support—ARMS!
Centre—FACE!
Forward—MARCH!
File—RIGHT!
Outward countermarch in single file—MARCH!
Inward countermarch—MARCH!

The same by two's and four's.

Outward countermarch in circles, by sections—MARCH!
Forward—MARCH!
Outward countermarch in circles, by platoons—MARCH!
Forward—MARCH!
Into line—MARCH!
Carry—ARMS!
Order—ARMS!
REST!

ATTENTION!
Shoulder—ARMS!
Support—ARMS!
Carry—ARMS!
Trail—ARMS!
Shoulder—ARMS!
Order—ARMS!
Shoulder—ARMS!
Present—ARMS!
Shoulder—ARMS!
Charge—BAYONET!
Shoulder—ARMS!
Order—ARMS!
REST!

ATTENTION! *Shoulder*—ARMS! *Right*—FACE!
Sections, right into line—MARCH!
Company, forward—MARCH!
Right oblique—MARCH! *Left oblique*—MARCH!
Forward—MARCH! *Forward*—MARCH!
Right turn—MARCH!
Company, by platoons—MARCH!
By front of company—MARCH!
HALT! *Support*—ARMS!
Form cross on second section—MARCH!
Sections, left turn—MARCH! HALT!

March, in cross, by right and left flank.

Reduce cross and from front of company on 2d section—MARCH!

Right—FACE!
Forward—MARCH!
File—RIGHT!
File—LEFT!
File—RIGHT!
File—RIGHT!

Right by file into line, two paces distant—MARCH!

Carry—ARMS!

Order—ARMS!

Shoulder—ARMS!

Present—ARMS!

Shoulder—ARMS!

To the right close—MARCH!

Right—DRESS!

Order—ARMS!

Rest—AT EASE!

Let this be written out distinctly and practised thoroughly at this drill. Try nothing else, and preserve this order of arrangement. Let the commanding officer carry this paper in his breast and consult it when in doubt.

Whatever has been omitted may be displayed at the next parade.

UNIFORM, ETC.

There are reasons for the adoption of a permanent uniform, one to be worn every day, by a whole school. A boy who is dressed in the uniform in which he has been taught "the position of the soldier," will be constantly reminded to bear himself in a soldierly manner. He will be conscious that eyes are upon him as he walks the streets; and he may overhear such remarks as, "There goes one of the Cadets!" If he has learned that "a perfect soldier must necessarily be a perfect gentleman," he will remember and do credit to his instruction. He will not, generally, engage in such rough-

and dirty amusements as are likely to injure or soil the uniform which he is proud to wear. He will feel manly, and will behave like a man. Of course not *every* boy, but *most* boys, will be thus influenced.

The expense, to each one, for an every-day uniform, should be less than for the usual variety dress. The cloth chosen, and the necessary trimmings, can be bought at wholesale, from "first hands," and any tailor will contract to make the clothes of a company, and to continue making them, at a less price per suit than he would ask for a single suit.

Many of our best schools have adopted a permanent uniform, and their teachers and parents are pleased with the results.

If such an uniform is to be procured, I may advise a grey suit, trimmed neatly, and not over-trimmed, with black silk braid; or a suit of dark blue, trimmed in the same way. To the taste of many, an entire suit of one color is more pleasing than a suit of which the coat is of one color and the trowsers of another. It will become a question, also, whether all shall wear coats, or all jackets. I have seen both styles, and my own taste has been better pleased with the coats. I have preferred little boys in short-skirted coats, to large boys, of sixteen or seventeen, wearing jackets.

The summer trowsers of either uniform may well be of white or brown linen, which forms a pleasing contrast with either blue or grey.

The coat should be single-breasted, and cut with a military collar. The trimming on the coat may be only on the collar, (except for officers, see below,) and on the trowsers, a plain stripe on each leg.

The regular army buttons may be ordered, in quantity, through any tailor.

The army "fatigue cap,"—a style much worn boys,—may be very cheaply purchased by the and oiled-silk coverings may be bought with them.

The entire uniform, thus described, need not cost more than $10 to each one, and may be procured for less. However, it will not be economy to buy cheap cloth for a permanent uniform. At wholesale prices, good grey cassimere may be bought for from fifty to sixty cents per yard.

Thus dressed, the officers may wear a little gold lace. Corporals are entitled to one "chevron"* of gold lace on the left arm; sergeants to two; lieutenants to three; and the captain to four. Sergeants may have a narrow strip of lace around their caps; lieutenants two strips; and the captain a band of broad lace, extra gilt. The three commissioned officers may wear epaulettes on parade. A pair of good gilt epaulettes, good to wear and last, will cost about $4; cotton epaulettes, which may well take the place of gilt ones, will cost seventy-five cents a pair. Epaulettes are fastened on the shoul-

* A "chevron" is a strip of gold lace sewed on the arm above the elbow, in a V shape, the angle of the figure being uppermost.

der by passing under a band of gold lace; and this they should wear at all times, as they wear also the chevron. If they have neither, they should be allowed to wear a parallelogram of lace on each shoulder.

If it is decided to adopt a uniform only for parades, and if economy is a necessity, no expense, or next to none, need be incurred. Almost every boy has a dark coat, with gilt buttons. Secure, then, as much uniformity in dress as possible, (let all wear caps,) add a little gold lace, and, perhaps, a little scarlet trimming, and you have all that is really necessary.

If, however, the expense is not much regarded, a very pretty and very cheap uniform may easily be procured. Since the suit is to be worn only at occasional parades, it is not necessary to have cloth of any more than medium quality; the inside trimmings may be cheap, pockets omitted, and the sewing substantial but not of the best. Such an uniform, bought at wholesale, cut out by a tailor, but made by a tailoress, or at home, need not cost more than $6, cap and all, for privates, and $7 for officers.

Although this plan *seems* the cheaper, the other—of wearing a more expensive and durable uniform all the time—will be found to cost less "in the long run."

Guns are expensive. They may be procured at wholesale stores in New York at various prices, but at not less than $5 each, for decent arms. Possibly the teacher may be so situated as to be able to obtain, from the State authorities, the use of the "U. S. Cadet muskets," or the shorter (and clumsier) artillery musketoon. If this is possible, it certainly is advisable. But I would urge that guns are unnecessary. A very good imitation of a gun may be cut from seasoned oak or hickory, stained in imitation of black walnut and varnished, by any wheelwright or carpenter, and furnished at a cost of less than a dollar each. By some plan, bayonets may be procured, and fastened on these wooden guns. Thus equipped, the company, at a little distance, might seem to carry real guns.

For my own company, I provided these wooden guns, ornamented with the cast-off and polished up bayonets of a military company in town. My boys were contented with them, and some people "always thought that they had regular guns."

But I can recommend *lances* as being, in many respects, the best "arms" for a boy-company. They are cheap, neat, and have "no ugly, sharp points about them." They may be turned from ash, varnished, and tipped with a brass spear-head, and even ornamented with the "red, white and blue" ribbons (for parades) at a cost of from fifty to seventy-five cents each. For these (or for wooden guns) there should be a small knob of some kind, corresponding with the trigger-guard of a gun, by which they may be supported easily, and at a regular height.

Swords, for officers, may be procured from New York,

at various prices. A good sergeant's sword may be bought for $2 50 ; swords for the commissioned officers should cost a little more, but not more than $5 each. Belts cost about seventy-five cents each. Sashes are of two kinds, silk and worsted : those of silk cost about $5 ; of worsted, from $2 to $3.

Let us see, now, at what cost a company of thirty-two may be equipped. The uniform consists only of similar dark clothes and caps. In this case, the privates need expend but fifty cents each for lances, and a trifling assessment for the drum and fife. If the cheapest of everything must be bought, swords may be found at less prices than those above mentioned, say for less than two dollars each. We will have everything as cheap as possible, as follows :

4	Sergeants' swords and belts, . . .	$7	00
2	Lieutenants' " "	4	00
1	Captain's " "	4	50
3	pairs Epaulettes, at 75c.	2	25
24	Lances, at 50c.	12	00
10	yds. Gold Lace, at 30c.	3	00
	Drum and fife, ...	6	75
		$39	50

We may safely say, then, that a company may be decently equipped for $40. Now, from my own experience, I can advise a teacher to pay for all this himself, if, of course, he is teaching a private school. He may consider the money as an investment in his business, and I can assure him that it will prove a *good* investment. His school will be made so much more attractive, that he may safely calculate on receiving a sufficient increase of patronage, within six months, to bring back the money.

But whether the teacher buys these equipments himself or not, it has been demonstrated, I think, that the cost need not deter the teacher from attempting to introduce the system into his school.

The music for a company may be provided in accordance with circumstances. All that is *necessary* is one small snare-drum and a fife. If it is possible, let these be played by boys. It will be cheaper to employ instruction for them than to hire regular musicians at every parade. It is advisable to equip the musicians in a style somewhat different from the rest. Scarlet jackets look well; scarlet caps will cost less. They are to be under strict discipline, like the rest, to be present at all drills, and to learn just when and what to play.

The flag may be home-made. If made and presented by young lady friends, it will be the best possible. Flags of various prices are for sale at the military stores in Maiden Lane, New York, costing from $10 to $100. Send the amount of money you can afford to expend, and a flag of that value will be returned.

There should be an *armory* of some kind, in which the guns or lances, the swords, flag, drum, &c., should have suitable places. If nothing better can be procured, a rack for arms may be cheaply put up around the sides of the school-room.

PLATE I.

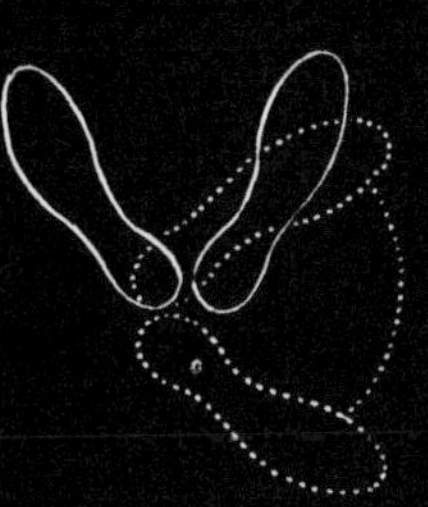

Right Face.

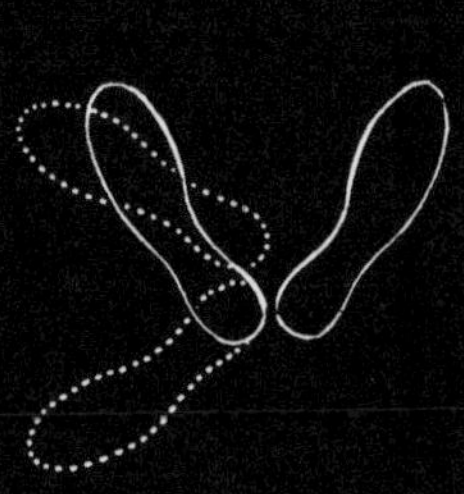

Left Face.

Rest.

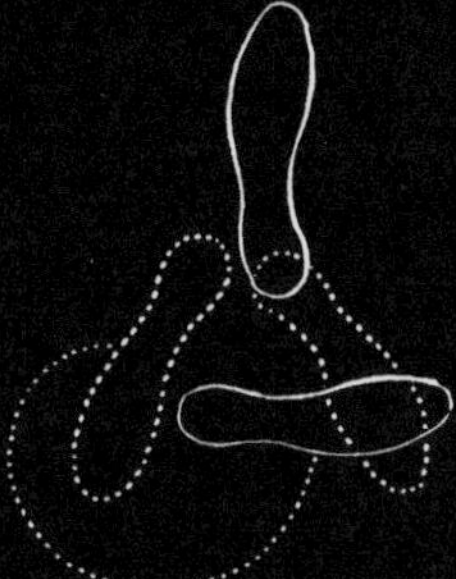

About Face.
Whole Line; About:
dotted Line, Face

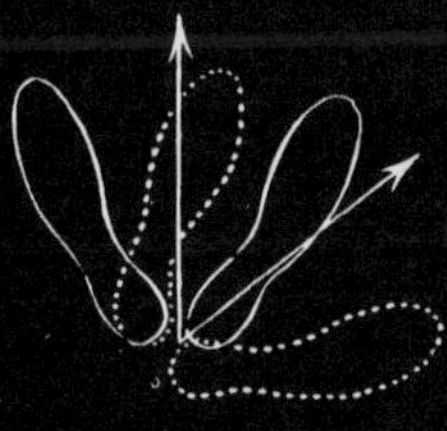

Left into Line.

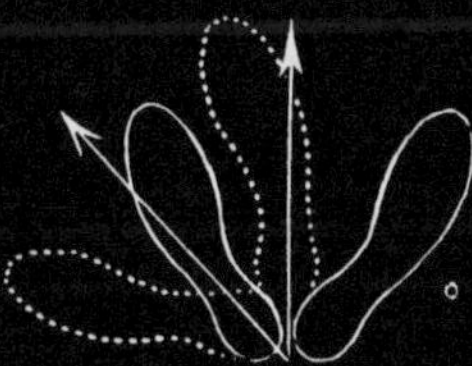

Right into Line.

Engraved by J.W. Barber. New Haven Ct.

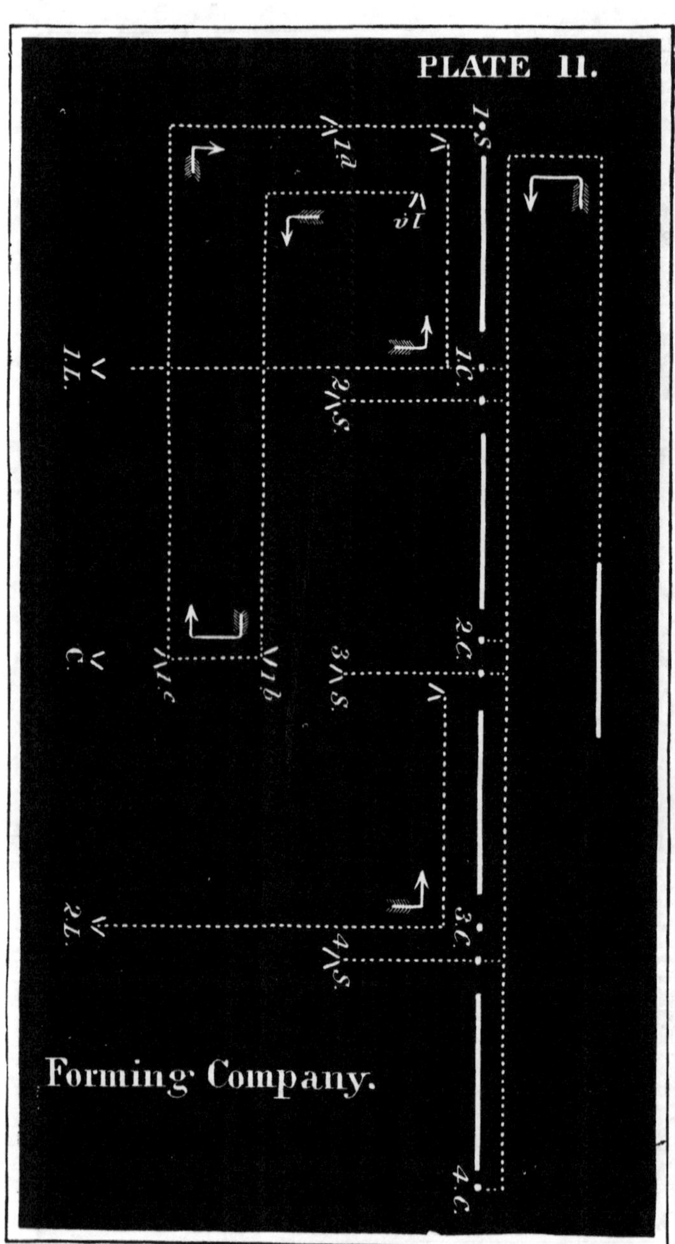
PLATE 11.
Forming Company.

PLATE III.

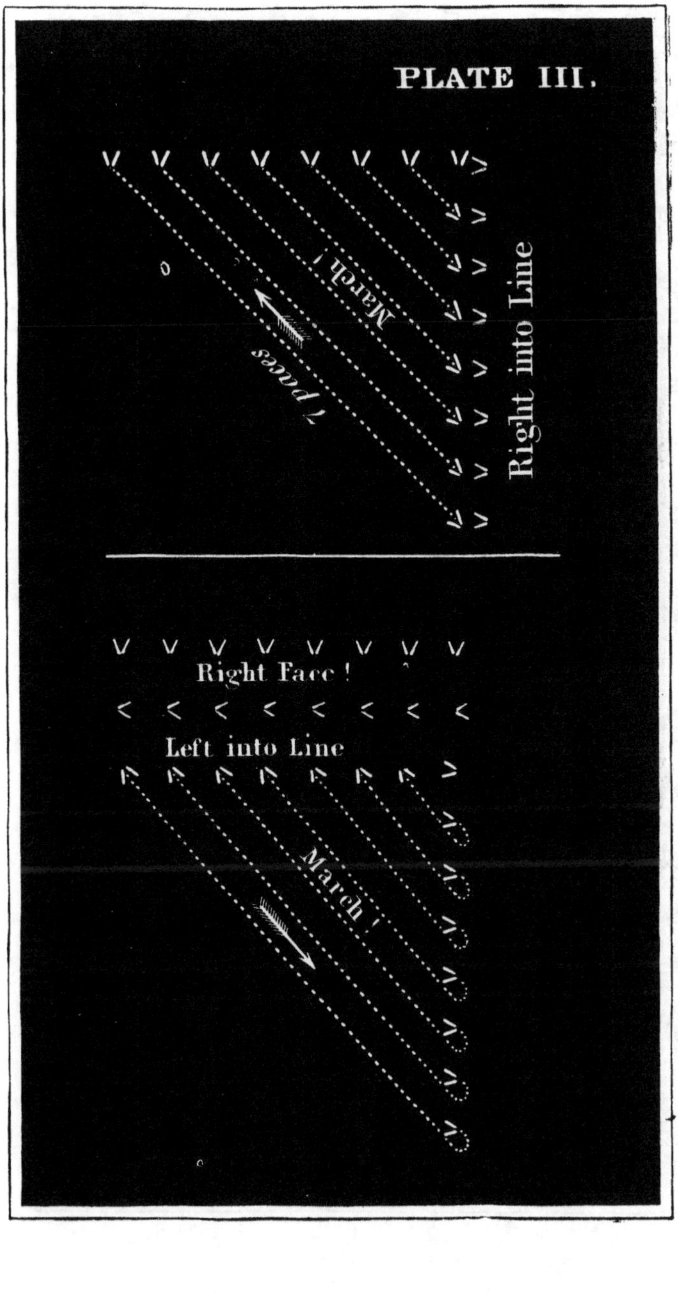

Right into Line

March!

7 paces

Right Face!

Left into Line

March!

PLATE IV.

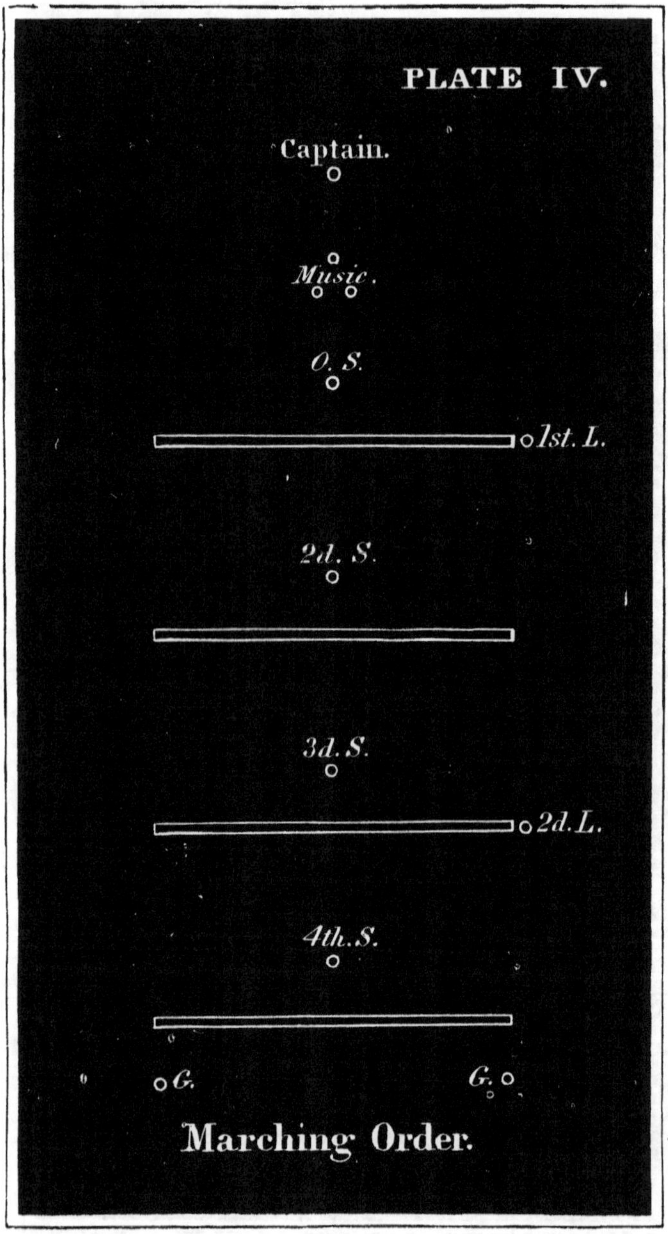

Captain.

Music.

O. S.

1st. L.

2d. S.

3d. S.

2d. L.

4th. S.

G. *G.*

Marching Order.

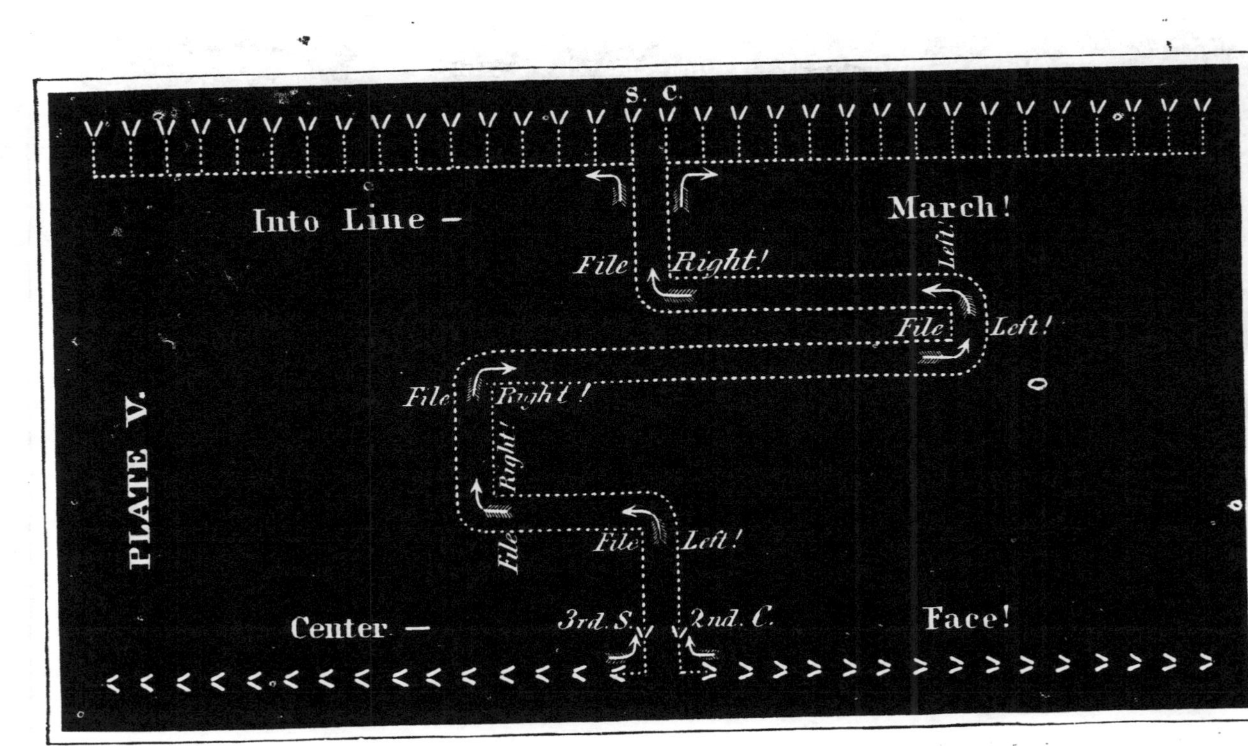
PLATE V.
S. C.
Into Line —
March!
File
Right!
Left!
File
Left!
File
Right!
Right!
File
File
Left!
Center —
3rd. S.
2nd. C.
Face!

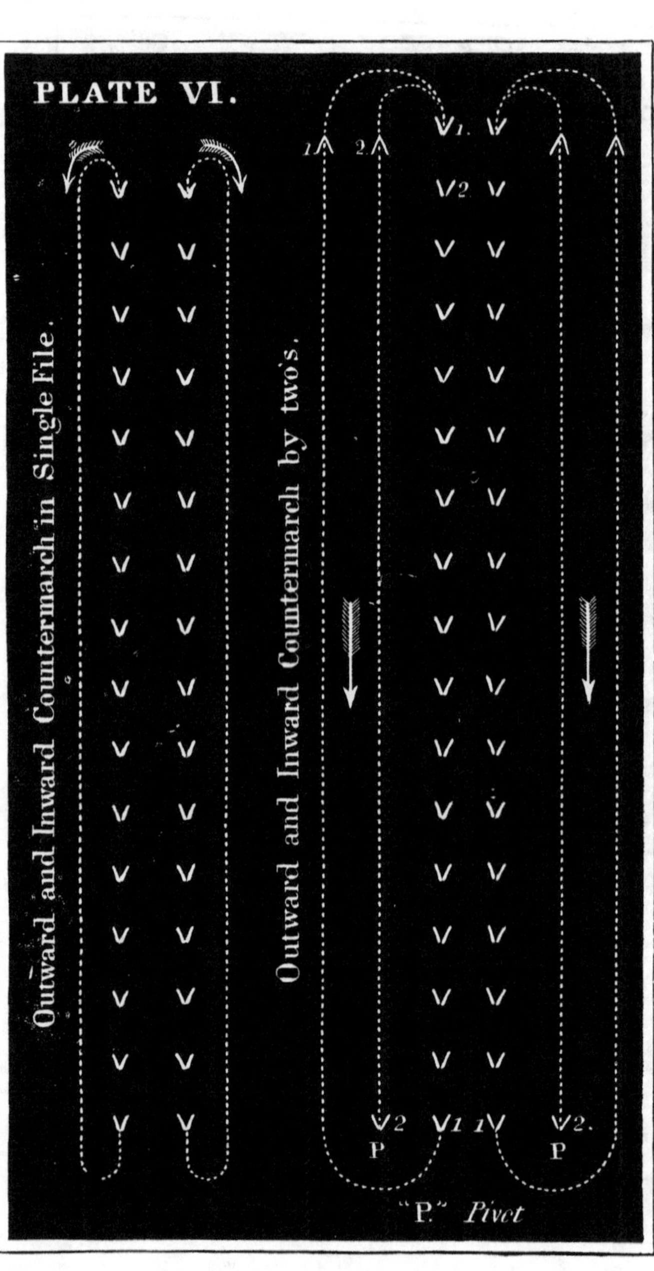
PLATE VI.
Outward and Inward Countermarch in Single File.
Outward and Inward Countermarch by two's.
"P." Pivot

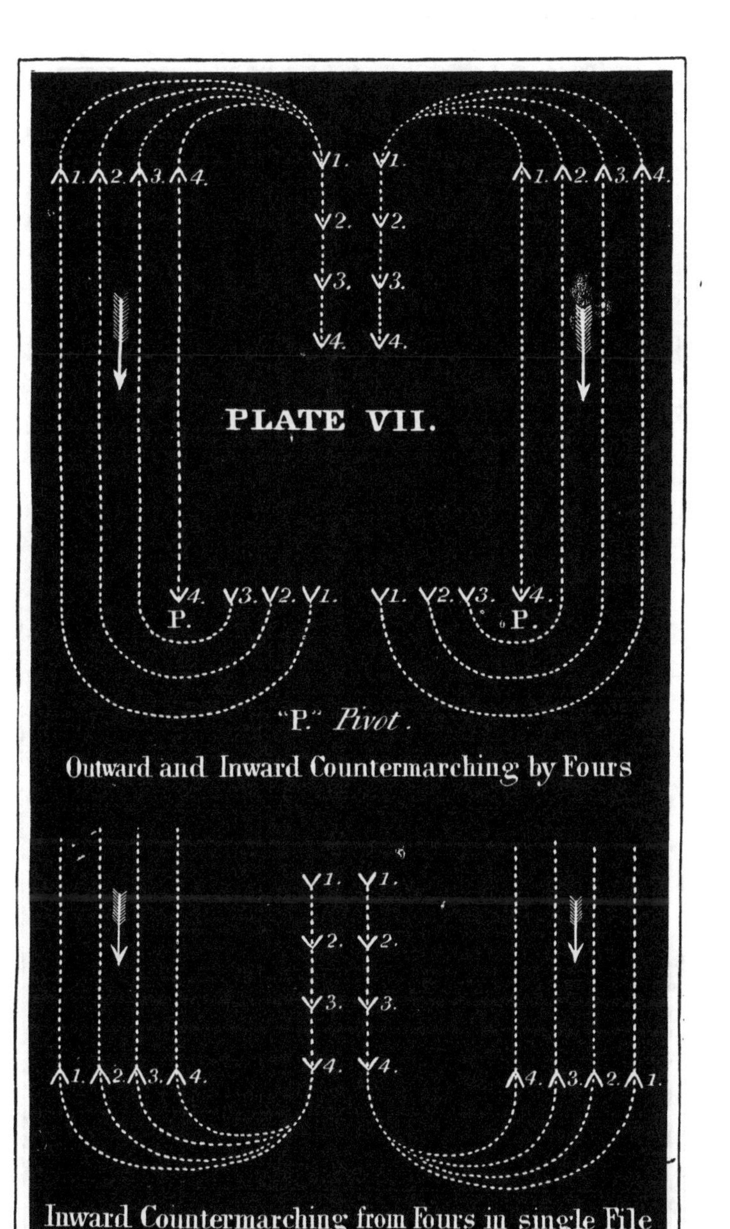

1. 2. 3. 4.
1. 1.
2. 2.
3. 3.
4. 4.
1. 2. 3. 4.
PLATE VII.
4. 3. 2. 1.
P.
1. 2. 3. 4.
P.
"P." Pivot.
Outward and Inward Countermarching by Fours
1. 1.
2. 2.
3. 3.
1. 2. 3. 4.
4. 4.
4. 3. 2. 1.
Inward Countermarching from Fours in single File

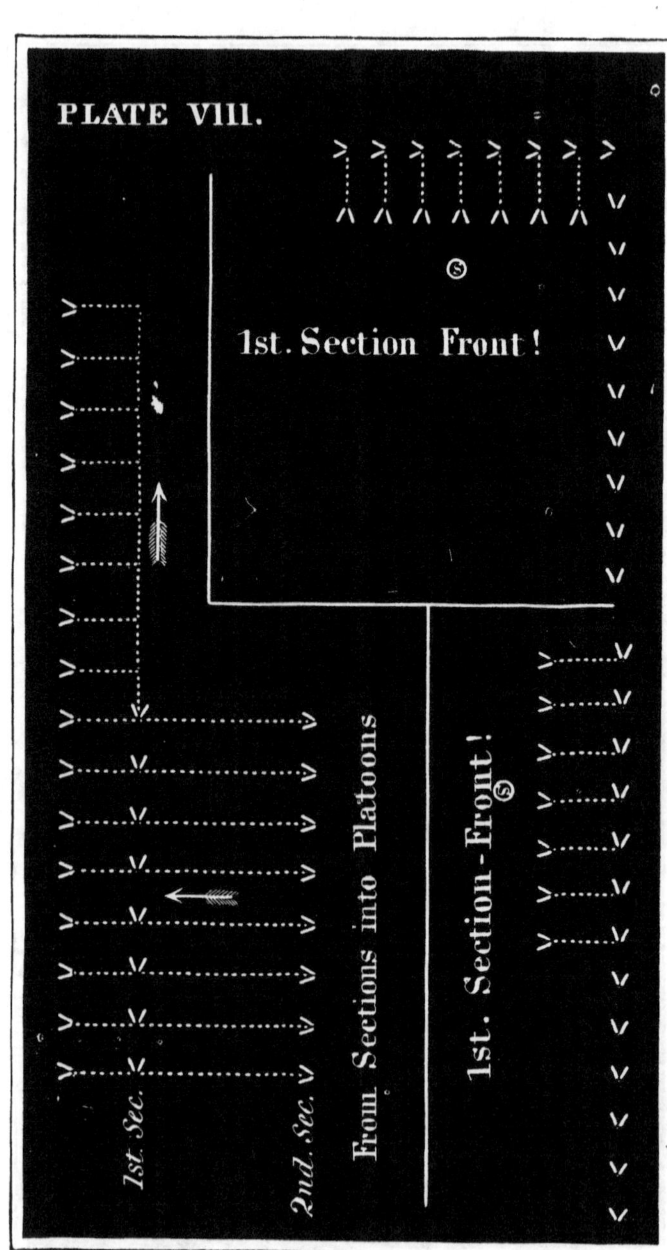

PLATE VIII.
1st. Section Front!
From Sections into Platoons
1st. Section-Front!
1st. Sec.
2nd. Sec.

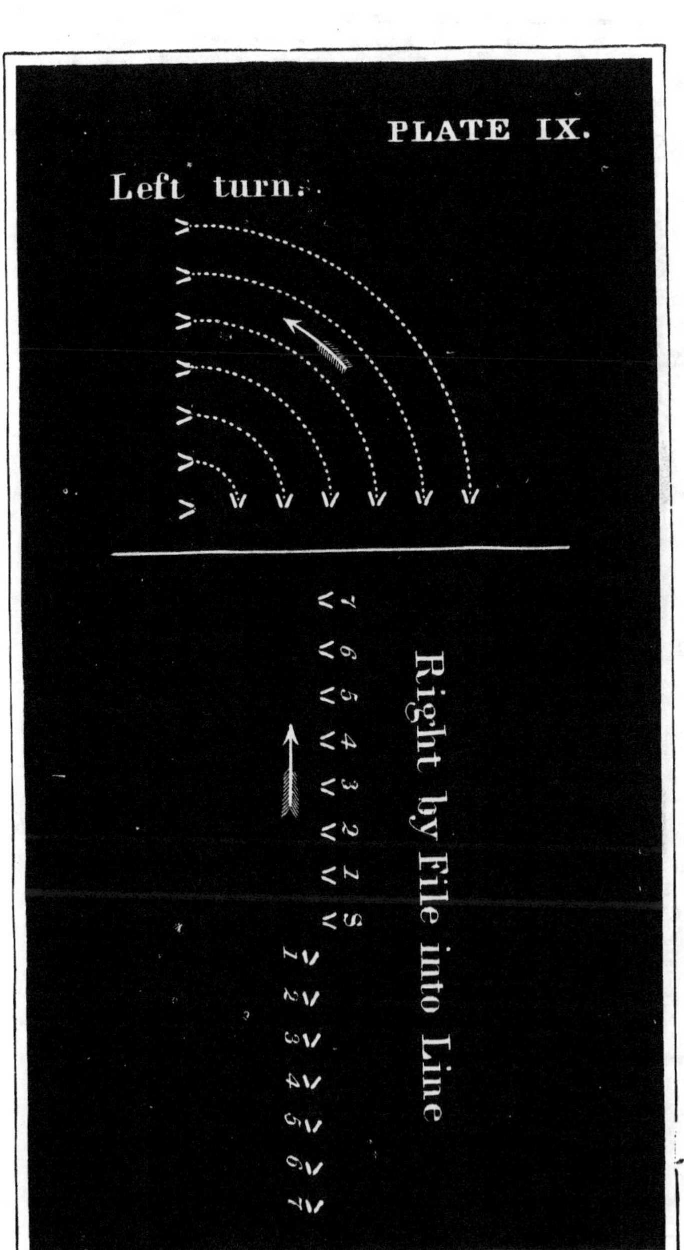
PLATE IX.
Left turn.
Right by File into Line
7 6 5 4 3 2 1 S
1 2 3 4 5 6 7

PLATE X.

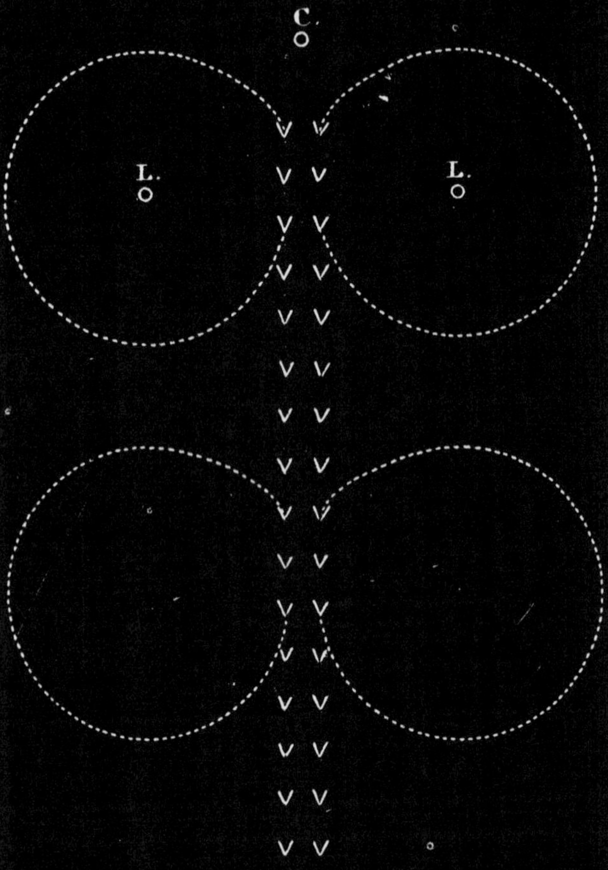

C.

L. L.

Outward Countermarch.
in Circles by Sections.

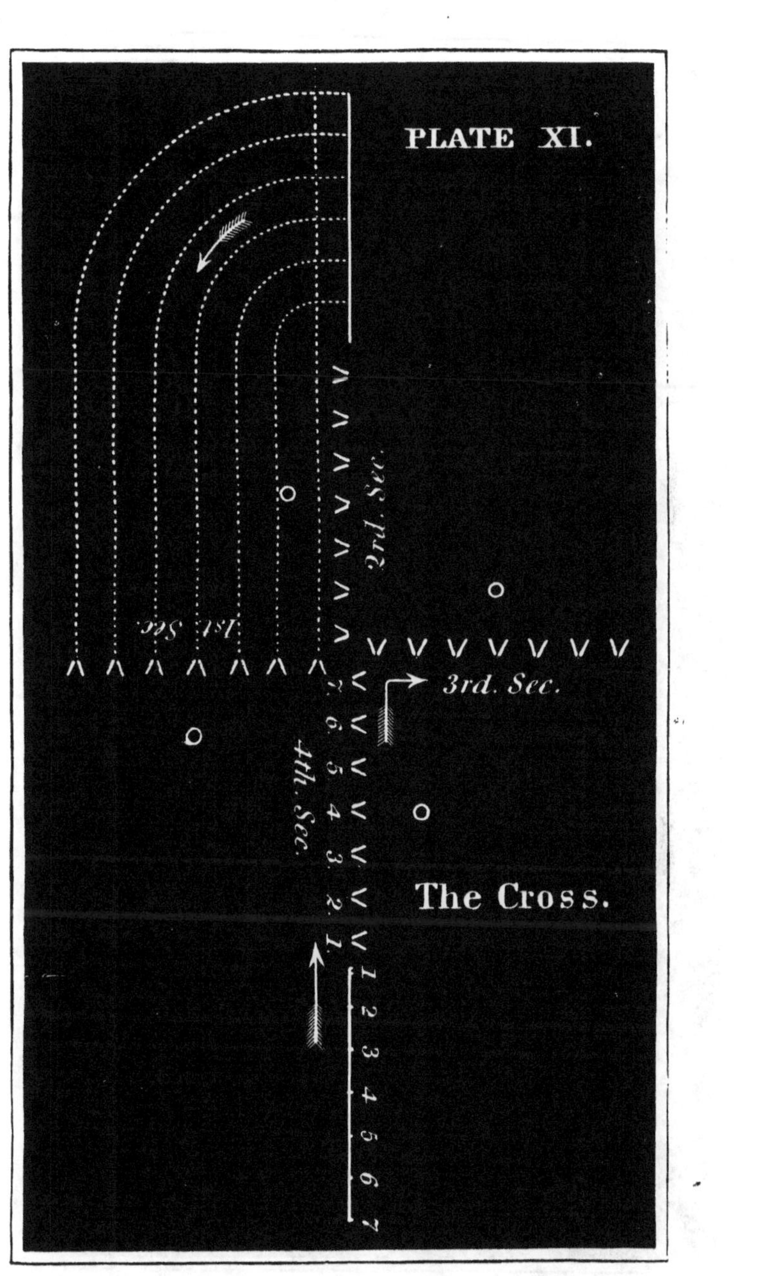

The Cross.

PLATE XII.

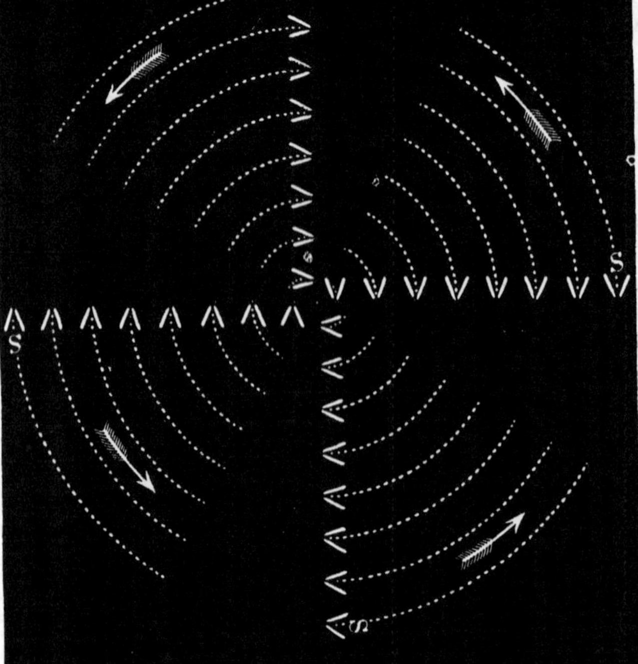

"Left turn"- in Cross.

PLATE XIII.

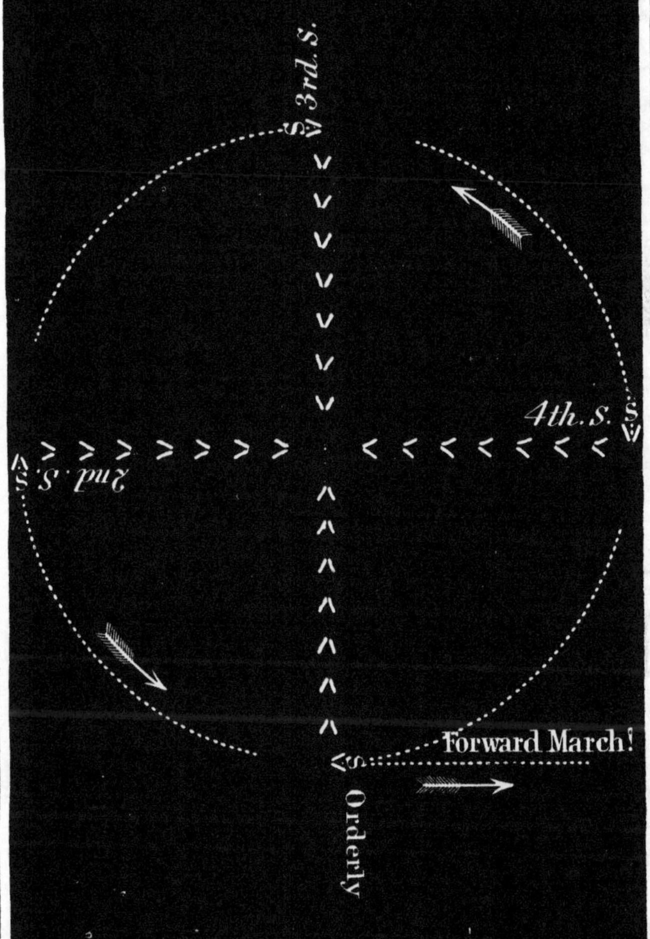

3rd. S.

4th. S.

2nd. S.

Forward March!

Orderly

Reducing Cross.

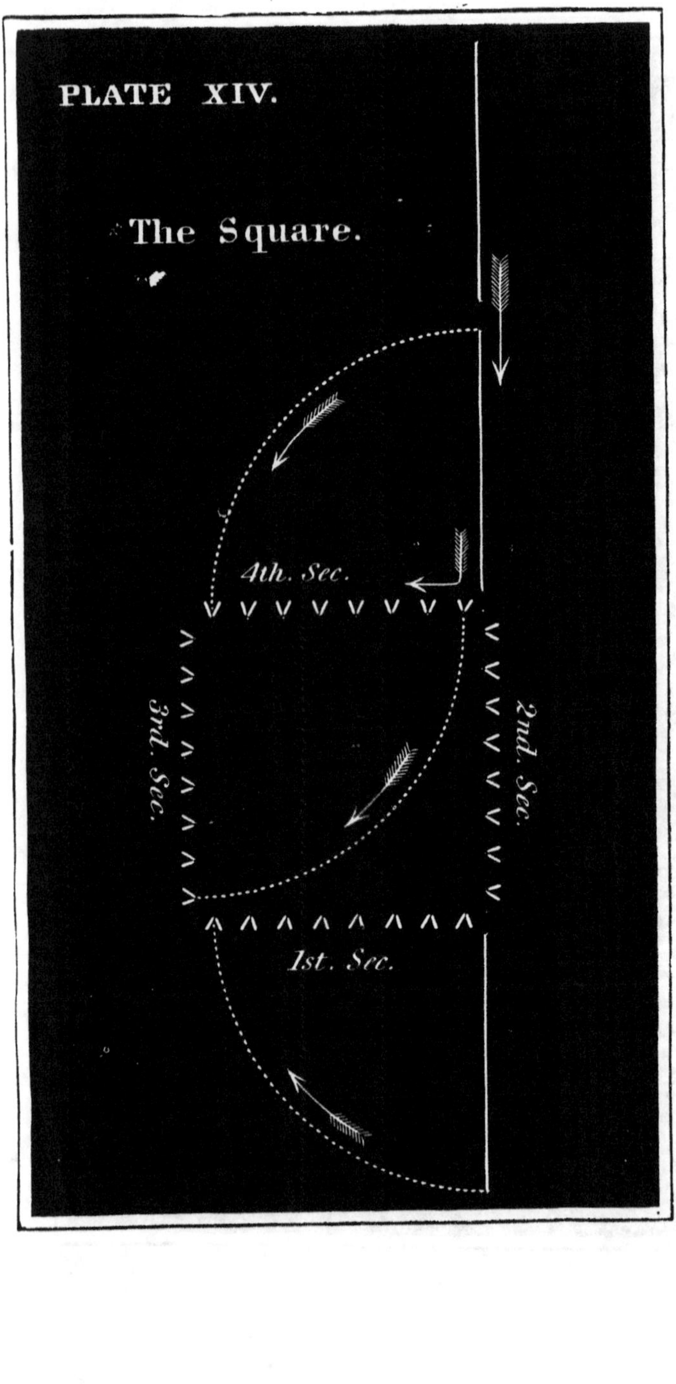

PLATE XIV.

The Square.

4th. Sec.

3rd. Sec.

2nd. Sec.

1st. Sec.

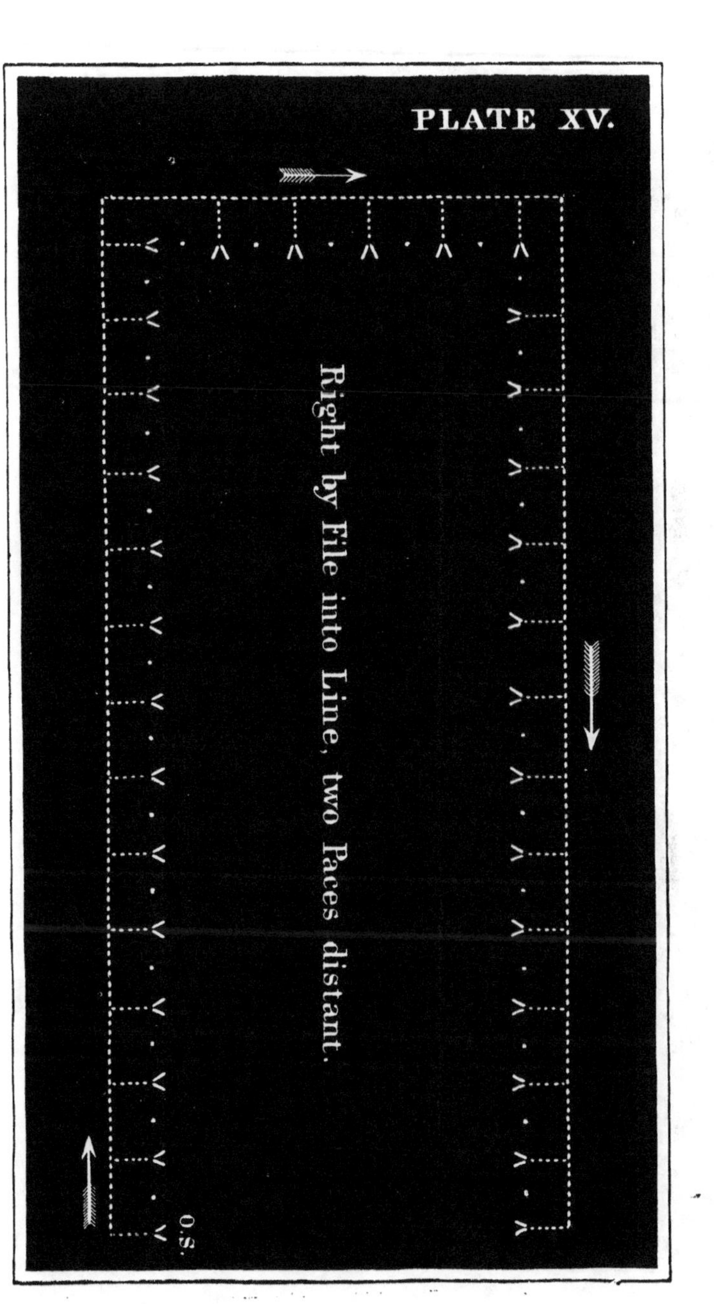
PLATE XV.
Right by File into Line, two Paces distant.
O.S.

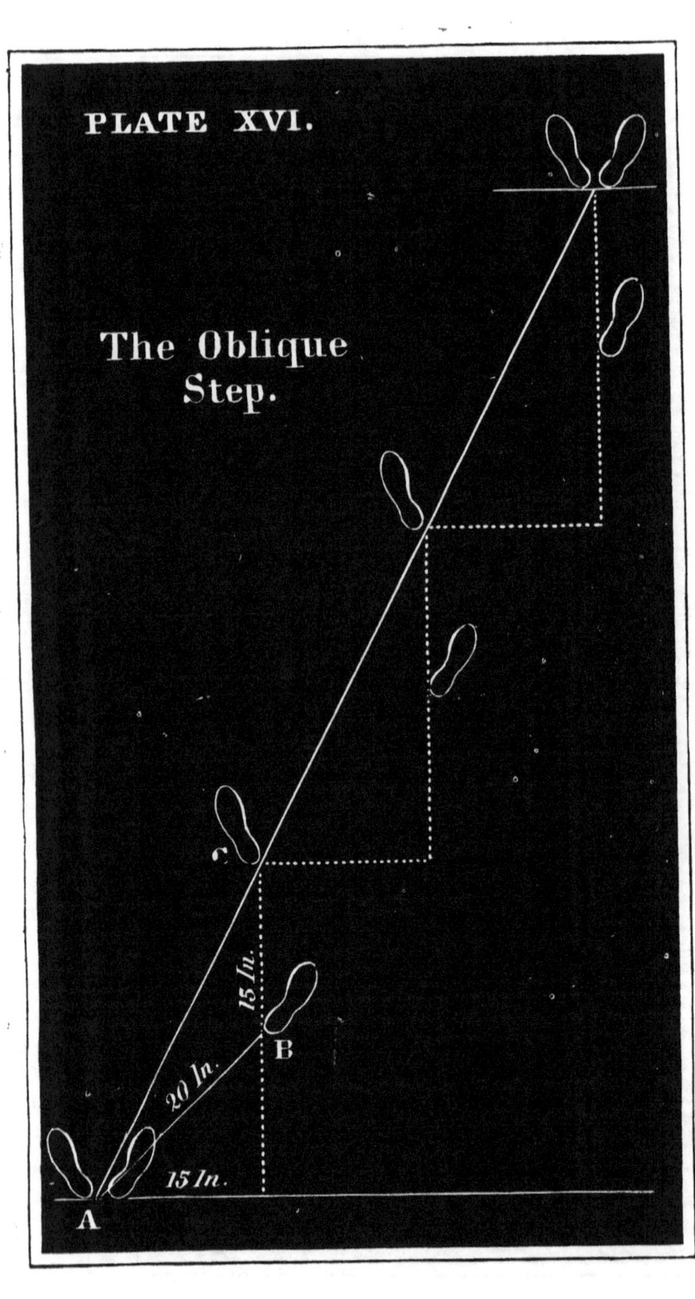
PLATE XVI.
The Oblique Step.
15 In.
B
20 In.
15 In.
A

GYMNASTICS.

INTRODUCTION.

It is a fact not sufficiently noticed and lamented, that the young men of this country, who are engaged in commercial or professional pursuits, are, as a class, but weak and effeminate specimens of manhood. We see them on their way to or from the counting-room, the office, the study, dragging along their half-vital frames, pale-faced, dyspeptic, sacrificing themselves to gain a fortune which they may not have life, and certainly will not have health, to enjoy if obtained. Moreover, there seems to be a strange prejudice against bodily exertion, and this, to such an extent, that he who has means on which to live without labor, takes a kind of pride in doing absolutely nothing. Fast horses and fast yachts attract a few, it is true, but the above assertions are not to be denied in their application to the majority.

The contrast between young America and young England, in respect to physical development, is marked and striking. One sees in the young men of England or Scotland most noble examples of robust, athletic and graceful manhood. The young nobleman and the poor barrister, the banker's clerk, and even the shopman, are, as a general rule, broad-chested, fresh-colored, hearty fellows, who take pride in walking ten miles before breakfast, in pulling a pair of sculls as well as a regular wherry-man, or in being thorough sailors, able to trim a sail or clean a deck. Athletic sports of various kinds are cultivated by the people.

It will not be denied that we, as a nation, are unwise in neglecting the admitted necessities of amusement and exercise; but it will not seem out of place here, the repetition of some of the arguments in favor of physical education.

1. Nature demands it. Boys, at least up to the time that their heads reach the level of a counter, and they breathe in the lowest stratum of our polluted business atmosphere, delight in nothing so much as play, and that the heartier, the better. During that period nature demands and receives her full meed of attention; the muscular and digestive systems, so closely allied, work harmoniously together; the mind grows with the body, and under proper intellectual care, they seek mental and physical exercise with equal avidity. But as soon as the *toga virilis*, the skirted coat, is prematurely assumed, they "put away childish things." Their stock of boy-health and vigor lasts

for awhile, but too soon, the *love* of mental exertion, (its twin companion, bodily exercise, having been put to death,) passes languidly away, and the spurs of ambition or desire of gain must be used to urge on the slow paces of a half-vital existence.

2. Active exercises confer beauty of form; and they even contribute to impart an elegant air and graceful manner. The most perfectly-formed man I ever saw was a young merchant, who was, at the same time, an enthusiastic gymnast; a sculptor would have rejoiced to copy his graceful form, and study the details of his magnificently developed muscles; he walked the streets with the carriage of a Grecian hero. And yet this same man had been by no means conspicuous for manly beauty before he began a course of training; he had, in fact, entered a gymnasium in accordance with the advice of a physician, who wished to drive away incipient consumption. In this case, daily ablutions in cold water accompanied the exercises of the gymnasium, and now, although he no longer labors at the vaulting bar, he values his bath more than his breakfast, and is like a caged lion if deprived of his regular daily exercise. And he accomplishes almost the work of two men in his business, yet keeps up with the literature of the day.

His is not a solitary case: I know of many such, but not enough.

The Oxford and Cambridge students afford numer-

ous examples of the *mens sana, in corpore sano*. Read Bristed's "Five years in an English University," and admire the manliness of the sensible students there.

Recall the beauty of the heroes of the Grecian warriors, or of the contestants in the olympic games, as wrought in the living marble of the old sculptors, or copied by the genius of Flaxman. The Greeks were *men*, and all the more heroes, and statesmen, and scholars, for *being* men.

3. A *consciousness of* strength and dexterity, naturally leads a man to noble efforts in the defence or preservation of the weak or helpless. He who has been taught to be fearless in the water, and has learned to rely on his strength and endurance of muscle, will leap boldly into the waves to rescue a drowning person, while a score of sickly, effeminate fellows will be trembling on the shore. In many other ways, which need not be mentioned, true courage will be found to be allied with a consciousness of power, gained by actual experience in manly exercises.

If these things be true, it becomes us, as teachers, to inquire how we may best use our influence over those committed to our charge, to make them *men*, to implant in them a fondness for manly, healthful exercises, to give them a thorough education, physically as well as mentally.

In answer to this question, I beg leave to call the earnest attention of teachers to my descriptions of the

following branches of physical education, which I offer as the results of considerable personal experience and long attention to the subject, as displayed in books and the practices of some of our best schools.

Drilling—so called—has been already treated of, and there remains to be said but little on that subject. It has been considered mainly as a means of interesting students in their school and teacher, of teaching principles of subordination, unanimity, and promptness of action, an erectness and grace of carriage, and of affording an innocent way of occupying time, likely to be otherwise misspent. But drilling may be also regarded as a branch of physical education. The boy who maintains "the position of a soldier" through a long drill or parade, at the same time carrying a musket of a weight by no means to be despised, gains strength and endurance of muscle, together with a certain degree of activity, and a habit of alertness and energy of motion.

I am free to confess, however, that the tendency of drilling, unaccompanied by other exercises, is to give lads a certain stiffness of body which is by no means to be admired. French soldiers, who are taught, most thoroughly, a great variety of gymnastic exercises, are celebrated for their activity and cat-like litheness. In ranks they can be as immobile as statues, but in action they are as agile as leopards, and their powers of endurance have been attested by their rivals, yet

inferiors, the English soldiers, in the late Russian war.

It is necessary, then, I submit, to combine with drilling any or all of the exercises which are treated of hereafter.

The teacher will remember, also, that the usual games and sports of boyhood ought not to be discouraged. Bat-ball and foot-fall, "base" and "tag," and similar sports are well adapted to boys; but while clinging to these, they may yet be initiated into more manly exercises, which may soon take the place of "childish things."

It may be well, at this point, to speak for a moment of the old notion that the teacher loses dignity by mingling with his scholars in the amusements of the play-ground. I am glad to have evidence for believing that this impression is retreating before the light thrown now-a-days on the profession of teaching. The teacher who is in doubt in regard to this, has only to try the experiment of joining in the sports of his boys to be convinced that he may, if he will act judiciously, maintain his dignity in the school-room, a dignity supported by the affection of his pupils, although, on the play-ground, he may have acted as the companion, and even the equal of his young friends. If he will but be *the elder brother* or *kind father* of his boys, leading and guiding them in their studies and sports, he will be acting as a true teacher. The days of the mere school-*master*, let us hope, are nearly over.

I come now to speak, in course, of the following exercises, viz.:—

Walking, running, skating, swimming, archery, rowing, and exercises particularly confined to the gymnasium. I may here willingly confess my indebtedness for many suggestions, to that excellent English work, "Walker's Manly Exercises," an American edition of which, I may add, has been recently published in Philadelphia.

CHAPTER I.

PEDESTRIANISM.

It may be remarked, at starting, that too much attention is apt to be given to the development of the muscles of the arms and upper part of the body, to the neglect of those of the lower limbs. Viewing the matter practically, it is evident that there occur frequent instances in which the legs are called upon for prompt, rapid, and continued action. In self-preservation, or the rescue of others from accidents in the water; in pursuit after, or flight from, those whom circumstances render the enemies of ourselves or others; in journeys, or in forced marches, in which, as, for instance, in the case of Lieutenant Strain's party on the Isthmus of Panama, life may depend on the speed or endurance of one man; in these and other similar circumstances there may often happen a need for stout legs, strong in large muscles, and guided by a thorough knowledge of what legs can do.

In addition to these considerations, it may be well observed that the laws of grace and symmetry demand that the muscles of the *whole* body shall be developed and strengthened. The brawny-armed blacksmith stands, likely enough, on a pair of "spindle shanks," while the postman, or the professional dancer, has stout legs, but puny arms and a weak chest.

GENERAL DIRECTIONS.

Exercise of any kind is best practised in the early morning, or towards night, and if indulged in during the day, it should never immediately follow a meal.

All unnecessary clothes should be laid aside, and the limbs left perfectly free. It is advised, particularly, that the habit be formed of leaving the chest and throat exposed; at least the practice so much indulged in by boys, of wearing "comforters" around the neck, should, except in very cold weather, be discouraged. The same advice applies to the covering of the head; during exercise, a straw hat, or light oiled silk cap, is best.

Many recommend a belt, tightly strapped around the abdomen. When used, however, it ought not to be strapped *too* tightly. In walking, and in other exercises not violent, the belt is unnecessary, but in running and leaping, and similar exercises, a moderately tight belt answers the purpose of preventing the too violent motion of the viscera, and of supporting the organs of the chest.

Exercise should always begin gently, and end in the same manner. The being cooled too quickly is injurious; therefore a sudden transition from action to rest, drinking cold water while hot, and lying on the ground, should be avoided. As soon as the gymnast ceases his exertions, he should resume his clothes and continue walking about, moderately, until thoroughly cooled, or until ready to begin again. Men take this same care of race-horses, and they show singular folly if they neglect themselves.

As preparation for walking or running, there are various exercises for the legs, tending to strengthen their muscles. Some of these are,

1. Standing with the left foot in place, and taking a long step in advance, with the right, bringing the foot back to place promptly.

2. Standing with the right foot in place, and stepping with the left.

3. Standing perfectly erect, and practising any of the "facings," as taught in drilling.

4. Executing the peculiar stamping movement used in fencing, instructions in which are contained in any Boys' Own Book."

5. Standing on one foot, and holding the other in various forced positions.

It is advised that these be practised in line—simultaneously, in obedience to commands—by a regularly formed class.

The suggestion might have been previously made that it is advisable to form classes for all exercises, and this for reasons obvious to every teacher.

A circular "course" should be laid out in the playground, or, better, in some large, open field. If nothing better can be done, measure off a course in the highway, between two piles of stones. Let this course be as smooth and free from stones, &c., as possible. Let it be measured in sixteenths of a mile, or in rods, and devise some plan of distinctly displaying the degrees of distance—by means of stakes, or marks upon a fence, parallel with the course.

WALKING.

In walking, it is not expected that speed will be attained. Good walkers very seldom accomplish more than five miles an hour, although for a single hour, and even for two and three hours, a pace of six miles an hour has occasionally been kept up. It is not desirable for an adult to attempt more than four miles an hour for any long excursion or trial; and at that rate he can walk comfortably from morning to night.

Boys, of course, cannot accomplish as much, but there are few of them, over twelve years of age, who cannot make three miles an hour, for a long walk, and four or four-and-a-half for a single hour. Strength and patience to endure, is that which a pedestrian needs at first, to try to gain. After he becomes accustomed to walking, he will come in from a walk of ten or twelve miles before breakfast, as fresh as when he started, the blood coursing in every vein, and with an appetite like that of a horse, while the lazy fellow who has crawled from bed just in time for his morning meal, has little enjoyment of food, or spirit for the labors of the day.

The walker will not, of course, confine himself to "the course;" he will delight in country walks, over fences and across lots. And the teacher will do well to organize excursion parties for his whole school, all starting off to see how far they can walk in the afternoon.

RUNNING.

The teacher may find it difficult to create an interest in walking, except among his elder pupils; but all will become enthusiastic about running. Enthusiasm naturally accompanies ardent efforts to excel, and is, also, stimulated by this vigorous exercise; for excitement of body always produces excitement of mind.

Taking advantage of this desire to excel, let the

teacher form classes and offer, in each, "the champion's belt" to the fleetest or most enduring,—a belt made well and slightly ornamented. Besides this, it will be well to honor the champion of the school. Races may be arranged, in which, by giving a start to the younger or shorter boys, the conditions may be just to all. Occasionally, therefore, let all compete together. Let the champion wear his belt until some one surpasses him and gains it.

Directions for Running.

In beginning a course of training, the racer should not allow himself to run until he is completely out of breath. He should begin with short courses, and, as he makes these gradually longer, he will find his lungs grow strong by exercise, and he can ultimately run a distance, to have accomplished which at first, would have been impossible.

Let him learn to keep the mouth firmly closed and to breathe only through the nose; to respire slowly, filling the lungs completely at each inspiration, and retaining the air in the lungs a moment before letting it escape. He will be astonished to find that, by such practice, he can become "long-winded," and will realize other advantages from having a large and strong pair of lungs.

In running, let the arms be held firmly at the sides,

the fore-arm held so as to form an angle rather acute at the elbow, and let the hands be clinched. If the arms are allowed to swing, their motion interferes with the momentum of the body. Let the body be inclined forward, the shoulders and head thrown back.

After passing the running post, it is best to keep on running a few rods, and to keep in motion for some time after completing a course. Too sudden a change from violent action to complete inaction is hurtful, because the artificial heat created by muscular exertion passes off so rapidly as to cause colds and rheumatic complaints.

For a long course, endurance, or "bottom," as it is called, is of more worth than fleetness. Great speed is called for only in short matches.

For boys of ten or twelve, two hundred yards, *at full speed*, is quite far enough. This distance may, of course, be increased for older boys or young men.

For a race to test endurance, let a long course, from half a mile to two miles be tried; or, let the contestants attempt to pass over the longest possible distance within a given time, say from ten to thirty minutes.

Feats in Running.

A mile in ten minutes is good running. A thousand yards in two minutes is *very* good speed. Six hundred yards in one minute is *extra* fast.

Ten miles an hour is done by all the best runners. A mile in four minutes has, perhaps, never been accomplished, but it has been done in four minutes and a half; while a mile in five minutes is frequently made.

These feats have been accomplished by men; boys cannot do as much, but legs half as long as men's legs ought to do more than half as much.

SKATING.

It will be unnecessary to do more than call attention, briefly, to the merits of skating as a gymnastic exercise, and to speak of the best kinds of skates.

The muscular exertion demanded in skating is similar to that made use of in walking and running; but since the exercise is taken in cold, bracing, wintry air, and at a season, also, when the number and variety of out-door sports is limited, it has peculiar claims on our attention.

It may be said that boys need no instruction in skating, and the remark is quite true. The subject is treated of here because it is the aim of the writer to induce teachers to take interest in *all* the amusements of their pupils, and this in such a way as to gain and retain an influence over them for their good. I have one other reason; I wish to persuade teachers to enjoy, themselves, the vigorous exercise and healthful warmth and lightness of mind and body consequent upon an hour's skating in the bracing north wind.

Skates are of various kinds, and it may be said that the simplest in construction are the best. The ornamental curl which, for its grace, is much admired by boys, is a useless and, sometimes, a dangerous appendage. It adds to the weight of the skate, and is liable to catch against dead branches, which may happen to be on the ice, and thus trip the skater; besides this, if the foot catches in an air-hole, or breaks in, the curl prevents an easy release.

The runner should be as low as possible; if it is high, too much exertion will be required from the muscles of the leg in keeping the ankles stiff. The best height of runner is about three quarters of an inch, and the width from an eighth to a quarter of an inch.

Grooved skate-runners are much used in this country, while in Holland, where skating is a national exercise, "flat-bottoms" are universally preferred. For beginners, grooved runners are of use, because they take a firm hold on the ice and prevent that spreading apart of the legs which is the young skaters first trouble. But for those who have passed through their initiation of bumps and troubles, who are at their ease, at home, on the ice, the Dutch pattern is the best. With these, all the intricate "rollings" and cuttings of graceful figures which mark the skillful skater, can be easily performed. This kind of skate can be easily kept sharp, for they can be ground on a common grindstone.

The bottom of the iron should be a little curved; much more ease and grace of motion may be acquired with curved than straight bottoms. The curve of the iron should be an arc of a circle whose radius is two feet. This shape enables the skater to turn his toe or heel outwards or inwards with equal facility.

The heel of the shoe or boot worn by the skater should be low, so as to permit the whole foot to come in close contact with the skate and thus be fastened firmly to it. Heels are an excresence of modern shoes; they are unnatural and would be extremely awkward were we not accustomed to them from childhood. For skaters the rule should be—only heel enough to hold the peg; and if the wood is thick enough, cut away that part on which the heel rests and file down the peg, so that the bottom of the foot shall be parallel with the surface of the ice.

Beginners may be taught to balance themselves on their skates by practising walking on them in a room, the floor of which shall not be dirty or gritty, and thus spoil the edge of their runners. I have seen beginners make excellent progress by retaining a hold of a long cord, fastened to a post or tree on the shore, or a stake made fast in the ice; by means of this they pulled themselves forward, so that the arms exerted the propelling power, giving the feet a better chance to learn the peculiarities of the stroke.

Dangers in Skating.

"If the chest is irritable it is neither salutary nor easy to skate against the wind. In countries where these exercises are general, inflammations of the chest are very common in winter.

"Skating sometimes exposes to much danger. If the skater find that he cannot get away from rotten ice, he must crawl over it on his hands and knees, in order to reduce his weight on the supporting points. If he fall at length on weak ice, he must roll away from it towards ice more firm. If he fall into a hole, he must extend his arms horizontally over the edges of the unbroken ice and only tread water till a plank is pushed towards him or a rope thrown for his hold." (Walker's Manly Exercises.)

From these few hints and instructions, the teacher, although not a practised skater, may gather information which, with other acquirements in similar exercises, shall tend to give him that influence over his scholars, both indoors and out, which he may and ought to have and retain.

SWIMMING.

The writer was once saved from drowning by the fearless action of a friend, who leaped into the water in full dress, and rescued him at the last moment. I is not strange, therefore, that he feels as if he were only discharging a part of the debt which he owes to his fellow-men, in urging on all the acquirement of the noble and healthful art of swimming.

If swimming should be taught in all our schools, to both boys and girls, how many lives might be preserved! It is true that boys generally learn to swim, and that without instruction, but they practise the art merely as an amusement, and only they who are naturally daring and energetic become sufficiently expert and fearless to afford reliable assistance to others, or to save themselves, in circumstances of danger. But it must need little, if any argument to prove that all may profit by suitable instructions, and by practice in various methods of swimming—with or without clothes and weights, alone or grappled by others, &c., &c. And it is submitted here, that it is the *duty* of teachers, a duty which they owe to humanity, to teach swimming to their scholars, to prepare them for the accidents which they are so likely to meet, during life, on the water. While they are fulfilling this duty, they will be, at the same time, instructing their scholars, and adding to the general reputation and success of their schools.

Confidence.

A great reason why boys do not learn to swim easily, why they do not generally acquire a practical and thorough acquaintance with the art, is because they lack confidence.

In the first place, the uncertainty and unknown depths of the water naturally alarm them. They are about to trust their life to an element which is proverbially treacherous. They fear the dark holes which may be waiting to swallow them down to a dismal and horrid death.

In the second place, they are not assured of the fact that their bodies will naturally float. They fear that they shall sink, and as soon as their feet are off the bottom, in an effort to swim, they make convulsive efforts to support themselves. These efforts teach them nothing. Swimming is only to be learned by slow and regular attempts in moving the arms and legs. During these hurried, frightened, and vain efforts to sustain themselves in the water, their heads, which they do not know is the heaviest part of their bodies, naturally gets under water; they become blinded and half suffocated; their terrors are increased, and they, at last, scramble out, more than ever convinced that the water and their bodies are natural enemies.

The confidence they need may be easily given to them by a teacher who has read the following, or other instructions, and who enters systematically on the business of teaching the art.

Time.

In the Northern States, the season for bathing extends from the middle of May to the middle or end of September. The danger of entering the water too early in the season should be explained by the teacher. Boys are anxious to "go in swimming" by the first of May, during those warm spring days, when they become heated by exercise. But at that time they have not left off their winter clothes, their warm undergarments, and the change from being warmly clad to nudity and contact with cold water, is greater than they think for. My father used to give me this rule: Don't go into the water until a week after you have left off wearing your under-shirt.

Morning is a better time for bathing than evening. It is not advisable to enter the water before digestion is finished. One should *never* bathe while in a perspiration; it is unwise even to undress while perspiring freely, unless in very warm weather, and during the middle of the day.

Place.

Of all places for swimming, the sea is best; running water next; and ponds the worst. Whatever place is chosen, let the character of the bottom and the depths be accurately learned by all. Stakes may be driven to mark the line beyond which the depth is "over head." For diving, care must be taken that there is always sufficient depth, and that the bottom is free from stones.

Dress.

Due regard to modesty, in the case of a teacher and his class, requires that short drawers be worn by all. A little ingenuity and effort will supply them. If the bottom be stony or shelly, canvass slippers, no matter how roughly made, are desirable. Leather shoes become useless after a few exposures to saturation and drying.

Each scholar should have a suit of old clothes ready to be worn in the water, after sufficient progress has been made in plain swimming.

First Lesson.

Wet the head on entering the water. Avoid standing still long at a time, while naked, either in or out of the water. Let the instructor, followed by his class, wade cautiously all over the ground, in order that the boys may see that it is nowhere over their shoulders. Let all be convinced of this, so that no one shall fear getting beyond his depth.

Let the teacher now show his class the buoyancy of his body by floating; or, if he cannot float, let him illustrate the difficulty of keeping his body beneath the surface of the water. Let him explain why the chest is the lightest part of the body, the limbs next in density, and the head the heaviest. In salt water, one-tenth of the weight of the body will remain above the surface; in fresh water one-eleventh. If, therefore, the body can assume such a position as to leave above the surface the nose and eyes, for the sake of seeing and breathing, the swimmer may float at ease.

As an experiment in further illustration of the buoyancy of the body, let the beginner, standing breast-high in the water, attempt to bring up a handful of sand from the bottom. He will find it difficult to sink himself, although his head is under. Dr. Franklin advises the boy to try to bring up an egg, left purposely at the above depth. To accomplish this, he must go down with his eyes open. There is no trouble in doing this, if the experimenter will only *think* so. It is important for all to learn to use their sight under water, as, for instance, in cases where a drowning person has sunk, and a diver plunges down to bring up the body.

Require every boy to try to bring up the egg or sand. Let all learn in this lesson, first, that it is impossible for the body to sink, as long as the lungs are filled with air; and, second, that the place chosen is safe.

Aids.

In succeeding lessons, the first principles of swimming may be taught.

The aid of the hand is much better than corks, bladders, or any similar supports. Let the instructor offer his hands, held firmly just beneath the surface, as a support for the body of the pupil, one hand being placed under the chest, and the other under the abdomen. Hold the boy thus, urging him, at the same time, to trust himself fearlessly to your care. If he doubts your ability, you may easily convince him that *he* can hold *you*; that the water helps to sustain the weight. When he is quietly resting on your hands, tell him to draw up his legs, and kick them backwards, like a frog, but not violently. When he does this properly, instruct him in the proper motions of the arms and hands. Require all to take the same lesson.

For the next attempt, provide pieces of cork or light wood, about a foot long, and six or seven inches broad, fasten bands to these, so that they may be tied on the back; let one end, which may be rounded, lie between the shoulder-blades. To this cork or float, other pieces may be added, and be so arranged that, as the swimmer improves, they may be left off, one by one. If, with these, a pupil seems to find difficulty in learning, take him upon your hands, and teach him. But do not force them to learn; convince them that there is no danger, and they will not require force.

Respiration.

Let the pupils be advised to breathe slowly and regularly, and to *draw in* the breath at the moment when the stroke has just been given with the hands, and the head, therefore, is well above the water. If the air is inhaled while the hands are thrust forward and the stroke is given by the legs, the mouth will be so near the surface as to make it likely that water will be taken in and strangling ensue.

Coming Out.

As soon as the pupil feels weary, or becomes chilly and numb, he should come out and dress himself. It is strongly advised that friction be used before dressing; this restores the circulation of the blood, creates an agreeable glow, and strengthens the joints and muscles.

General Suggestions.

Directions for the various kinds of swimming are contained in almost any "Boys' Own Book," and in Dr. Franklin's works. It seems unnecessary to refer to these here, because they are for amusement more than utility. True, a person obliged to swim a great distance has occasion to relieve himself by resorting to the various methods of propulsion or rest; but these are easily acquired. But the teacher should encourage, and indeed require, practice in swimming with the clothes on; in leaping into the water, in full dress, from a height as great as that from the deck of a ship; in swimming with a weight on one arm; in supporting the body of a comrade, or carrying him to the shore; in avoiding the clutches of one of their number who may act as a drowning person would;* to dive and bring up a weight equal to that of a drowned person; to swim for a long time; to swim long under water; and all such practice as can be thought of, which will be likely to be of practical use. Let the boys be animated to excel in these respects with the hope of being better able to save their own and others' lives.

Cramp may be cured or relieved by thrusting the leg violently downwards, at the same time drawing up the toes. If this does not succeed, let the swimmer

* The method to be adopted in such a case is to avoid the fatal grasp by approaching the drowning person from behind.

turn upon his back and kick the limb out into the air, in which element he can make a more vigorous stroke. If this fails, let him support himself in an erect position, by the motions of the hands, until help comes. Persons liable to the cramp should never go beyond their depth.

Some bathers are much annoyed, and indeed, permanently injured, from water getting into their ears. This may be prevented by stopping the ears with cotton saturated with oil.

I cannot leave this subject without urging on the attention of parents and teachers the importance of accustoming the *girls*, as well as the boys, to the water. They are of the sex which is to *receive* aid, and they should be taught at least to become so familiar with the water as to retain their presence of mind in case of accident on the water, to sustain themselves, and to swim also if possible.

MISCELLANEOUS EXERCISES.

If the teacher will bear in mind that one great object which he has in view, in engaging in and superintending the sports of his boys, is to afford them innocent and profitable occupation for hours which are too often worse than misspent, he will not think it unimportant to attend, briefly, to

ARCHERY.

If he will assist his young friends, by his advice, in preparing bows and arrows, and targets, in making rules for practice, and, generally, in giving an importance to this exercise by starting and regulating it himself, he may easily succeed in making this one of the most interesting of the sports of the play-ground. The following hints may be of use :—

Bows are best which are made from seasoned hick ory, cedar, ash or elm. Their lengths should be equal to the heights of their owners. The string should be of linen, whipped with silk at the part where the end of the arrow is to be fixed. When strung, the cord of a bow five feet long should be five inches from the bow, at the silk.

Arrows are generally made from ash, birch or pine. For long ranges they should be about two feet three inches in length, for the largest bows. For target practice, the arrow should be longer and stouter. Plumed arrows are best. It is not difficult to plume an arrow. The feathers may be chosen from the smallest goose-quills, from the wing-feathers of hens, or from dove-feathers. If these are carefully and neatly fastened in the end of the arrow, the increased directness of its flight will pay for the trouble.

Targets may be made without instructions. It is

best to have two, and to fire from No. 1 at No. 2 till the ammunition of all is exhausted; then seek them and fire from No. 2 at No. 1. In this way no one need expose himself to being hit, and time is saved in going after arrows and returning.

There are two ways of registering shots: as "best shots" and "best average shots." Let

a	shot	within the "bull's eye"		count	ten;
"	"	"	1st circle	"	seven;
"	"	"	2d "	"	five;
"	"	without "	"	"	three;
"	"	striking on the edge		"	one.

Thus, if two boys make a match, and one hits the "bull's eye" (ten) and the edge (one) while the other hits within the first circle (seven) and within the second circle (five); the first makes eleven, and the second twelve. This seems the fairest way of judging of the relative skill of the two marksmen; for two fair shots are better than one very good one and one very poor one.

The distance from target to target may vary from thirty to fifty yards, for the larger boys; from twenty to thirty, for the smaller.

Shoot always with or against the wind; a side wind interferes with the course of the arrow.

It is suggested that a very pleasing public exhibition may be made of the proficiency of the boys of a school in pedestrianism and archery. Sensible parents will be pleased to see their sons engaged in such amusements, rather than herding together for mischief and profligacy.

ROWING.

Where boating is practicable, the teacher may find it desirable to have a boat club. Familiarity with boats, skill in rowing and steering them, and confidence and fearlessness on the water, are attainments which it would be well for every boy to make. The exercise of rowing is most healthful, especially since it is pursued in the fresh, open air.

The best boats, for six and eight oars, cost, in New York, from $150 to $300. A good four-oared wherry may be procured for from $75 to $100. But a large, flat-bottomed boat, may be procured for fifty dollars; if ornaments and paint are dispensed with, for less. These different sums, divided among a club of ten or fifteen boys, will not amount to very much for each.

Instructions in rowing cannot be easily given on paper. A few hours' practical teaching from a boatman or sailor will be worth more than pages of theoretical information.

CRICKET.

This English game, as yet not much played in this country, is worthy the attention of the teacher who seeks to add to the variety of play-ground exercises. It is the most popular of the athletic sports of England, and whether played by experienced hands according to scientific rules, or by a few lads, in a comparatively irregular manner, it is an admirable pastime.

The best rules for conducting the game, with both single and double wicket, with which the writer is familiar, are contained in the "Boys' Treasury of Sports," an English work, but which is republished in this country.

FOOT-BALL.

Strange to say, this excellent game is but little practised out of New England, but wherever it is known, it is a favorite sport.

Balls made from India-rubber are cheaper and better than the old-fashioned blown bladder, with leather case, but the latter is often procurable where the former is not.

In choosing sides, care should be taken that the larger boys be equally divided; upon them depends the impetus of strength and weight which frequently "crowds" or "rushes" the ball "to bounds." The smaller boys should act as skirmishers, leaving the brunt of the game to fall upon the heavy infantry.

Finally, the teacher may well interest himself in discovering and reviving old games, and in inventing new ones. "Strutt's Ancient Pastimes" contains many most amusing and interesting games, some of which are deserving of revival.

We now come to speak of Gymnastics, as exercises conducted with the aid of apparatus are commonly called.

GYMNASTICS.

We will first speak of the simplest forms of apparatus, such as are within the reach of the teacher of every village school.

The Vaulting Bar is the simplest, but one of the most useful, of the instruments ordinarily used by gymnasts. Upon it a greater variety of exercises may be practised than, perhaps, upon any other single "contrivance." It is easily constructed; the teacher who has any acquaintance with the use of carpenters' tools can make and put one up, with a few hours' labor.

In Plate I., on the left, are seen two of these bars; the details of their construction, together with instructions for their use, will be given hereafter.

On the right of the same plate is seen the Jumping Cord. It consists simply of two upright posts, firmly planted in the ground, with pegs of iron jutting from them at regular intervals, which sustain a cord; this is kept "taut" by the weight of bags of sand, fastened to either end. By this contrivance, the jumper, if he happens to hit his feet, will not trip, and the bags of sand can hurt no one, if the cord is carried forward violently by the unlucky or unskillful trip of the jumper. It will be seen at a glance that this piece of apparatus will cost less even than the Vaulting Bar.

With these two alone very many interesting and profitable exercises may be practised; and the scholars will thank their teacher for providing for them these simple and inexpensive means of enjoyment.

If the teacher wishes, he can add the Parallel Bars, seen on the right and in front of the plate, at but little expense. The upper bars need to be of hard pine, and planing is necessary; but a few dollars will cover the cost of them. For details of construction and use, see below.

Now there is not a teacher in the land who cannot erect one or all of these three aids to gymnastic exercises in his yard or play-ground. I wish I could induce all of them to try the experiment of introducing these exercises to their scholars. They would find, I am sure, that both their scholars and themselves would be profited by them.

Description of Plate I.

The apparatus here illustrated has been planned after considerable experience in various gymnasiums—experience in erection and practice. The whole is designed to be put up out of doors, compactly and strongly, and at the least possible expense. But little ingenuity is required to adapt the various parts to an indoor arrangement, if a suitable room is at the command of the teacher.

There are ten different kinds of apparatus, namely:

Two Vaulting Bars,
Upright Bars,
Single Rope,
Ladder,
Rope Rings,
Swing,
Inclined Board,
Jumping Cord,
Parallel Bars,
Horse.

These include the principal contrivances of our best gymnasiums. Others might be added, but at an expense increased beyond the advantages to be gained from them.

The whole expense should come within fifty dollars, and if the teacher is mechanically inclined, and will, with the assistance of some of his older boys, do most of the work himself, it may be made to cost much less.

Construction.

The main frame-work,—which is represented in the plate as being put together with hardly enough solidity and firmness, should consist of two stout posts, with a cross-bar. The posts should be deeply set in the ground, and may be rendered more firm by stanchions in various places. The uprights should be from fifteen to eighteen feet in height, and should stand at a distance of about twenty-five feet apart. The ladder, by being made fast to buried posts at the bottom, and screwed by iron clamps to the cross-bar, may be made to steady the whole frame-work, and prevent its swaying toward either side.

The perpendicular Parallel Bars, (on the left, within,) should be made of clear stuff, two inches in diameter, round and perfectly smooth, and twenty inches apart; they should be morticed squarely into the cross-bar, to prevent turning, and should be secured, in position, below, by being made to enter a stout piece of scantling, buried beneath the surface of the ground.

The Single Rope, which hangs next to these bars, needs hardly any explanation. It should be of a size just large enough for convenient grasping. It, as well as the other ropes, should be made to work on a hook, firmly inserted in the cross-bar, and connecting with it by an iron "eye;" by constant use, a rope, without iron gearing, will soon become so much worn as to be dangerous. The hooks ought to pass through the cross-bar, and be secured by "nuts" above.

The Ladder should be made of hard smooth pine, and be most solidly put together. It is the most expensive part of the apparatus, and may be dispensed with; and if given up, its place as a support of the frame-work may be supplied by a stout, smooth pole. There might be two of these poles, one on each side of the frame. The ladder should be inclined to the frame at an angle of 35° or 40°. It should be two feet wide; rounds should be small and smooth, and placed at a distance of fourteen inches apart. All angles and corners must be avoided in this and all the other parts of the apparatus.

The Rings of the next contrivance should be made of iron, six inches in diameter, and should hang about six feet from the ground. They may be covered with leather or by a waxed cord, wound evenly around them, or may be left, smoothly filed, of plain iron.

The Bar of the Swing, which comes next, should be of hickory, an inch and a quarter in diameter, and two feet in length. It should hang on a level with the rings. It is intended for the grasp of the hands, from beneath, and not as a seat. The ropes of both these swings may be shortened by means of knots, made fast by pegs.

On the inside of the right-hand upright, holes an inch in diameter may be bored, six inches apart, deep enough to admit stout pegs; these pegs should project far enough to serve as grasps for the hands, and should work easily in their holes. Two pegs are required, by means of which a strong-armed boy may hoist himself up, peg by peg, to the top, and come down again.

The Inclined Board should be made of two-inch stuff, about eighteen inches wide, and twelve or fourteen feet long. It should be planed perfectly smooth on the upper side. It is here represented as acting as a support to its end of the frame, inclining at an angle of 45°; but, if the frame can be made firm without it, it will be well to contrive means by which a less inclination may be secured. The use of this board is shown by the drawing in Plate IV.; from which it may be judged that the less the inclination, the greater will be the difficulty of climbing it. The ascent of a smooth board. standing perpendicularly, is not impossible.

The Jumping Cord has been already mentioned. In regard to the height and distance apart of the uprights, the teacher may exercise his own judgment. At distances of one inch, along the front face of both posts, short, smooth iron pegs should be inserted, projecting just far enough to sustain the cord, and not to interfere with its removal. Of course, the corresponding pegs of each post should be of the same height; and the distance in inches should be marked on both sides. Bags of sand are much better than any other weights to keep the cord taut, for, as has been intimated, the jumper may catch his toes against the cord, dragging it violently along with him, and bystanders are in danger of being struck by the flying weights.

The Parallel Bars (on the right and front) should be made of two-inch stuff, of the best clear, hard pine: the supports should be well planted, about four feet apart (in the length); the height of the bars from the ground should be about four feet; they may be ten or fifteen feet long, and seventeen inches wide, inside; the hand-rails should be rounded at the top, and be made so wide that the fingers cannot grasp or touch beneath.

The Vaulting Bars (on the left) should be supported by well planted uprights; the bars may be of ash or hickory, of two-inch stuff, worked perfectly round and smooth; one end at least should be morticed squarely into its upright. The bar nearest the main framework should be six or six-and-a-half feet high, and six feet long; the lower one may be a foot less in height and length. A third bar may be added, if a large proportion of the gymnasts are quite small. There are ways of arranging the bar so that it may be raised and lowered, for persons of different heights; but greater expense would be incurred if such plans were adopted, and that at a sacrifice of convenience. Where room must be economized, the movable bar is desirable.

The Horse—which is not a necessary animal in the

play-ground—should be made of a solid beam of well-seasoned wood, rounded at the sides, top and ends; it should be five-and-a-half feet long two-and-a-half feet in diameter, and the top four feet at least from the ground. The legs may be planted in the ground; but if they be made to spread, they need not enter the earth, for it will not be easy to overturn it. The handles, which represent the front and back of the saddle, should be very firmly fastened on; their shape and position are shown in the diagram in Plate IV.; they should be about sixteen inches apart. The seat may be padded with leather.

In the whole construction, the greatest care should be taken to have everything made as thoroughly as is possible. If accidents ever occur, let the teacher never have to blame himself for having been in any degree the cause.

Exercises.

It seems unnecessary to enter into details of instruction on the uses of these ropes and bars. If the more important feats of strength and agility are pointed out, and the *modus operandi* explained, the instinct which boys have for leaping and climbing will teach them all the variety which will be necessary.

It will be important that the teacher become able to take the lead in everything. Precept and example must go hand in hand, but example, in gymnastics, must be a little in advance. It will not be difficult, it is hoped, for a teacher to learn these exercises from the following instructions. Let him endeavor to show just how to do a particular feat; his pupils can imitate an action more easily than they can understand a description of it.

These exercises are designed to give strength to all the muscles of the body. It is true that more labor is furnished for the arms than the legs, but this is because the arms are more important than the legs, at least in many respects; and because, in exercising the arms, the chest, which contains the vital organs, is strengthened and expanded. To prove this, it will be interesting to take the measurement of the circumference of the chests of all of the pupils, passing the cord around just at the arm-pits, and to notice the gradual expansion which will be consequent on regular and vigorous exercises.

It will be appropriate for the teacher to give his class a lecture on the muscular system, and the physical necessity of exercise.

The first thing to be acquired is a good, firm *grasp* of the hand. This will be wanted in every variety of exercise. Let us begin, then, by attempting to strengthen the muscles of the fingers and hand. The parallel bars will give strength to the wrist and fore-arm.

1. Stand within the bars; grasp them with the thumbs

inside, and, with a slight spring, raise yourself so that the arms shall support the body. Try to do this *without* a spring, that is, by the mere stiffening of the arms. Your arms are not as strong as you thought. Now, keep the legs together and stiff at the knees, so that the body shall not sway about, and with the arms stiff, walk along the bars, stepping slowly, hand after hand.

N. B.—The teacher should allow only one thing at a time; he should forbid fanciful gyrations, and require each, in his turn, to perform the particular exercise which is the subject of the lesson; *after* the lesson they may do whatever they like.

As soon as walking forward is learned so well that all can walk easily and rapidly, try walking backward, standing on one hand, changing hands, *i. e.*, turning suddenly between the bars, and, before the body can fall, so that the feet touch the ground, face the other way. It is difficult but not impossible.

Try now the figures illustrated in Plate II. In The Grasshopper, lower the body slowly, drawing up the feet if necessary, until the elbows are on a level with the ears; now raise yourself entirely by the muscles of the arms. Do this as many times in succession as you can.

In making The L, let your feet be on the ground, stoop so that your arms can come outside the bars, take a firm grasp, draw up the legs to the position shown in the engraving, and remain so while some one counts ten, in seconds, and as much longer as you can.

The first position in Skinning the Cat is the same as for The L. The figure on the left illustrates the going over; the one on the right, the coming down. At this point do not let go, but, by a backward movement, turn over again without losing the hold. With practice, this may be repeated a dozen times or more.

While standing on the bars, swing your feet forward and backward. There is no occasion for fear. Swing far enough to turn a somerset, either forward or backward, but do not *make* the somerset; the feet, in coming down, might hit the bars too violently. This swinging prepares you for jumping. As the feet come forward, from a backward swing, let go with the hands, and allow the body to go forward. You may thus jump a foot at a time, and, with practice, a yard and a-half. Try jumping backward. Practise walking, swinging and jumping, while in the grasshopper position.

The upright parallel bars are for frequent use, from the first. Exercise in them tends to strengthen and expand the chest.

Stand with the toes just within the bars; grasp the bars in such a manner that the thumbs and fingers shall meet on the side opposite the body, and, in all the movements, retain this grasp and position of the hand, if possible. Now lean forward and pass the body through the opening, without moving the feet or letting the hands slip on the bars. Pass through, if you can ; never mind if it almost breaks your shoulder-blades. Now come back and repeat the movement. Go through and back with a *jerk.* This is capital exercise.

These bars, the single rope and the ladder, will give various exercises in grasping and in using the muscles of the arms. When working on either of these three, take care not to use the legs ; keep them stiff and straight. Ascend the bars with a grasp on each one, leaping up from reach to reach ; or climb one of them, without using the knees. It is a difficult, but by no means impossible feat, to ascend these bars with the head downward.

The teacher should encourage the invention of all kinds of difficulties. He should himself often offer the banter, "Do *this,* if you can !"

After the class has attained proficiency on the parallel bars, they may be taken to the vaulting bars. I will give, briefly, a course of lessons on these.

1. Grasp the bar with both hands, the thumbs on the same side with the fingers, and the back of the hand turned from you. Raise the feet, one at a time, by bending the knees and hang in that position, as long as you can. Try to sustain your weight, in this position, with one hand.

2. While hanging, move along the bar, backward and forward, by passing one hand over the other.

3. Hang by the hands, with knees straight and stiff, and draw up the body, by contracting the muscles of the arm, until you can hook the chin over the bar. Do this slowly, and repeat it as many times as possible. Bare the arms, and notice the effect of this exercise on the upper muscle of the arm. Improve on this by raising the body so high that the head and shoulders shall rise above the bar.

4. While hanging, draw up the feet slowly, and place them against the bar, between the hands; return to the first position, without losing the grasp. Do this again, but, this time, let the feet pass through the hands, under the bar, and without touching it, and come down on the other side, without losing grip. After practice and proficiency, pass the feet and legs through, but do not let the feet come to the ground; pause a moment, reverse the process and come back to the first position. This is called "skinning the cat," and is similar to the trick of the same name performed on the parallel bars.

5. Swing on the bar, so high that the feet shall rise above the level of the bar, both before and behind. Do this fearlessly, for your grip, by this time, will be strong enough to keep you from falling. Practice this frequently, since it gives confidence. As you swing

backward, let go of the bar, and catch it again as you come down.

6. Circling the Bar, is illustrated in Plate III. To accomplish it, draw up the body by the muscles of the arms, and while doing so, curl the feet over the bar, as seen on the figure. Do this by muscle alone, without a swing, if possible. When in this position, try to bring the feet so far beyond the centre of gravity on the other side, as to swing the body over and on the bar. Strength, and a certain "knack," are necessary to accomplish this feat gracefully and easily.

7. With a leap, throw one foot over the bar, and raise the body by the hands up on the bar. This is the "lazy way" of mounting the bar; the gymnast, who takes pride in his strength and skill, will always get on by "circling."

8. The Grasshopper (on this bar) is illustrated in Plate III. After mounting the bar, by either of the above methods, take a seat on it. Grasp the bar firmly, with the thumbs behind, and slowly slide from the seat as far as you can without losing the grasp. Return to the seat, raising the body by sheer muscle. At first, you may not be able to slip down more than a few inches, but, by degrees, you may gain strength and skill enough to assume the position of the figure in the plate.

9. As the body comes down in doing The Grasshop-

per, sustain it by hooking the elbows over the bar; grasp the dress at the thighs, firmly, and swing the body to and fro. After a time, you may succeed in swinging so well as to revolve around the bar a dozen times, or more, in succession.

10. Vault over the lower or lowest bar, at first with two hands, then with one. Go on to the high bar.

Note.—A "spring-board" is of use in vaulting. It consists of a stout hickory or oak plank, an inch and a-half thick, firmly secured to, and resting on, two pieces of scantling, two or three inches thick. By the aid of this, the "knack" in vaulting may be easily acquired, but it should not be used much by those who aspire to become great vaulters. With the spring-board, a good vaulter should clear a bar as high as his extended arms can grasp; without it, to clear a bar of the height of the vaulter's head, is good work.

Much attention should be given to vaulting, as it is one of the few exercises there are for strengthening the muscles of the legs.

The Swing, (on the right of the frame) is a vaulting bar, which is moveable. It is to be grasped from below. To obtain momentum, run at it, swiftly, and grasp the bar as you pass under. Of course this bar should be so high that one may swing from it without being liable to drag the feet against the ground. The knees should be bent up to prevent this. Continue to swing by a peculiar and almost indescribable exertion of the muscles; the feet must never assist by touching the ground.

While swinging and keeping up the motion, draw up the body to "chin the bar," as was done on the vaulting bar. Circle this bar in the same way. Let the swing be stationary, circle into a seat, come down as in "the grasshopper," and swing while hanging by the elbows.

While swinging, reach up and grasp the ropes; ascend and descend these, keeping the swing going all the time.

The Rings are a most important part of the apparatus. Strength of arm is necessary to use them.

See that the rings hang on, or a little below the level of your upstretched hands; place them so that their diameters shall be opposite to you; with a run, grasp them, and swing as high as possible, without ever allowing the feet to touch the ground. The trick of swinging by the hands consists, as nearly as can be described, in drawing up the body during the backward sweep, and, just at the point of turning to sweep forward, dropping the body so as to lengthen the radius which is describing the arc of a circle. An increased force is thus given to the pendulum, and at each such lengthening, the length of the arc is increased. The demand for strength is great, because, although one may have muscle enough to draw himself up, as described above, for a few times, yet to repeat-this long enough to attain the maximum, to describe an arc of 160° to 180°, calls for endurance of "mind" and muscle, which only the practised gymnast possesses.

Standing in the Rings, as illustrated in Plate III., may be learned while the rings are at rest, to be practised afterwards, while the swing is in motion. It is done with a slight leap upward, and, at the same moment, a stiffening of the arms; but regular gymnasts "get in" without a leap, by drawing up the body, and then, as it were with a kick against nothing, springing up and stiffening the arms.

The Grasshopper in the rings is shown in the plate, and needs no explanation. The gymnast should become dexterous enough to "get in," or "do the Grasshopper," while in full swing, and to change from plain to "fancy swinging," frequently and gracefully.

The Inclined Board, which should be as smooth as possible, should not be used with dirty shoes. With a wisp of grass, or a rag, rub off all gravel or sand from the soles of your shoes, before ascending. The illustration explains, perfectly, the method of ascent, which is by no means easy. The greater the inclination, the greater the difficulty of getting up. The writer has seen a perpendicular board ascended and descended in this way, but it is hard work.

There will be no need of giving instructions in the use of The Ladder. It may be remarked, however, that its object is mainly to test endurance. The going up and down once or twice, and by a round at a time, amounts to nothing, but the ascent by two, three, and four rounds, and the descent by six or seven, and this over and over again—these will try the muscles of the strongest.

At the Jumping Cord there may be leaping "with a run," from a spring-board and from the ground. The highest leaps may be made with the board, but real agility is best displayed by jumping from the ground. Begin with the cord at a height which you are sure of being able to clear, and advance by a peg at a time.

The Pegs afford a test of strength by no means to be despised, even by an experienced gymnast. Start with a peg in each hand; reach up with the right and place it in the highest hole you can reach; draw up the body by the right arm and enter the left-hand peg; continue this to the top; and descend in the same way. Ascend by every other hole, or every third hole, *if you can.*

The Horse is an expensive and not very necessary adjunct of our gymnastic apparatus. The illustration in Plate IV. shows one feat to be performed with this animal. It consists in jumping through one's hands. A firm hold is taken of the handles, and the gymnast jumps through and back again, without letting go. Other methods of performing on this quiet beast are, vaulting into the saddle over his head or tail, or from either side; taking so firm a hold on the handles, as to be able to sustain the body at a right angle with the arms and parallel with the horizon.

There are very many other exercises for these various ropes and bars which cannot be well described here. The teacher will find that his scholars will invent novelties every day. On his part he must adopt measures to excite and keep up an interest in the exercises. A good plan to accomplish this may be to recognize the "champions" in each variety of exercise, and to distinguish them by the insignia of—say, a red belt for the best leaper, a black one for the best vaulter, and so on. Let these belts, or other distinguishing articles of dress, be worn until some rival surpasses the champion and gains it for himself. Take care that the smaller boys be not shut out from competition; they should be allowed to gain championships in exercises which are within their powers.

PLATE I.
Engraved by J.W. Barber. New Haven. Con.

PLATE II.

The Grasshopper. *No.1.*

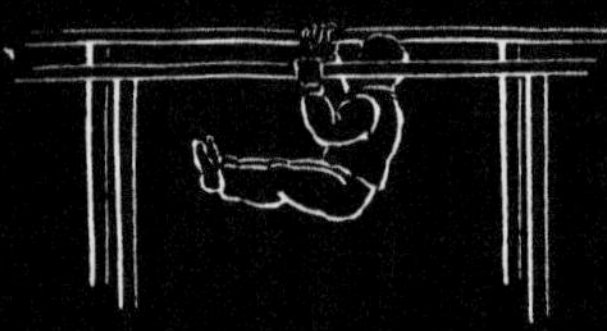

The L.

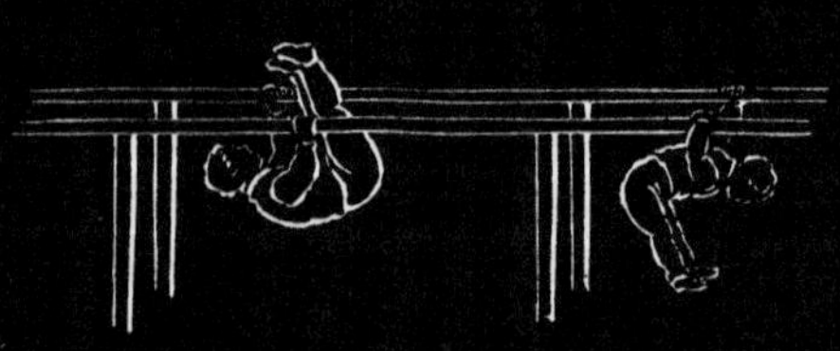

Skinning the Cat.

PLATE III.

Circling the Bar.

The Grasshopper. *No.* 2

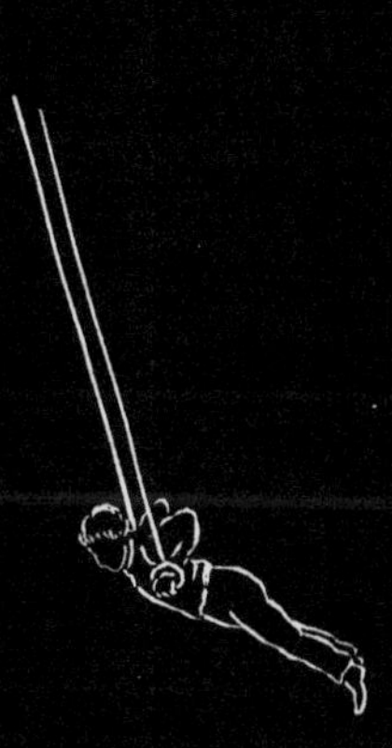

Grasshopper, *No.* 3.

Standing in the Rings.

PLATE IV.

The Horse.

The Inclined Board

The Long Reach.

SCHOOL MANAGEMENT.

We have thus far considered some of the ways and means for making the play-ground attractive and profitable; let us now come within the school-house. Much may be done here to carry out our design of "making school interesting"; and the teacher who undertakes and carries into effect the following or other plans for making his rooms cheerful and comfortable, and his daily exercise interesting, even sometimes amusing as well as instructive, will find his reward in his increased pleasure in teaching those whom he has caused to love as well as respect him, and in his success in accomplishing good—to say nothing of his growing popularity and more remunerative gains.

I have headed this section of my book "School *management*," and for a reason. I may illustrate the appreciation which is prevailing among latter-day teachers, of the idea contained in the italicized word, by telling a story, one which may be already well known, but which will bear repetition for its illustrative properties.

A farmer's boy was required, one pleasant spring day, to gather the stones which lay in a meadow and heap them together in the corner of a lot. They would be troublesome to the mowers, the farmer thought, and they disfigured his otherwise smooth "medder." The stones were quite numerous, and the task was no small one, but the boy began his labor cheerfully; he knew there was reason for the clearing, and, for awhile, he worked vigorously. But his back began to ache before long, and the merry shouts of some mates of his, who were playing not far off, on "the village green," began to annoy him. He was a Yankee boy, we may be sure, for his inventive brain soon devised a plan for saving labor and gaining time. He raised an old post in the corner in which his stone-heap was to be, and then left work and joined his friends. At a convenient moment, he threw a stone at a neighboring tree. "Who can beat that?" said he, as Fortune favored him, and his stone struck the mark. Immediately the others were aiming and hurling stones at the tree. But stones were not plentiful. "Come," said the young Yankee, "there are lots of stones over in our meadow; let's go over there and fire at a mark."

They were soon there; ammunition was abundant; the post in the corner was an inviting "mark," and by the time the boys had become wearied of this kind of sport, a large part of the work was done. The inventor then confessed his trick, and there needed but little urging to induce his friends to finish the "stent," and then all went off together to play at something else.

There are many points in this illustration which are worthy of study, and, making it a kind of text, we may notice that: 1st. There is *work* to be done in a school-room. The mental muscles are to be strengthened, and mental dexterity gained. The teacher's object is to educate and instruct his pupils, and to accomplish this he must make them *work*. To clear the meadow, a certain amount of actual hard work, and, in itself considered, of tiresome and unpleasant work, was necessary. Now, shall the teacher require of his scholars that they labor at the dull task of removing the stones to the pile, or shall he contrive some way whereby the labor shall be performed, yet be disguised as play? While the boy toiled slowly at his task alone, each stone grew heavier than the last, his back ached, and he thought more of that and of the distant shouts of his play-mates, and of how to "shirk" the work, than of the improvement which he knew he was making and the pleasure he was giving to his father. But when his comrades were around him, and the stones were flying, he forgot the task in the sport, he worked harder than he would have done and accomplished more in a given time than he would have done alone, and there was *pleasure* in the business.

2d. The boys who came to "fire at a mark" could not have been persuaded, probably, to come to help their friend gather stones into a heap. They were *deceived;* they went *cheerfully* to work without suspecting it to *be* work, and all worked harder than they could have been induced to work if they had entered on it as a task.

3d. Similar deception is not only justifiable but expedient on the part of a teacher in his school. He can and he ought to remove from school-duties their character of dreary drudgery, to make study pleasant and attractive. He need not make the labor less; in fact he will find, most surely, that his scholars will do more and work longer when work is made play, than when work is left mere work; and he may so lighten the hours that they shall fly by pleasantly *and* profitably, both to himself and to them.

4th. When the farmer's boy *threw stones at a mark,* "for fun," he worked harder than he did before. Boys always run farther and faster when playing than they can be easily induced to run on an errand. The *motive* makes the difference. And, in another view, labor is lightened when amusement takes off the attention from the task, as such. Sailors work better at the capstan with a "Cheerily O!"—the heavy anchor comes up more easily and sooner, and the men the sooner get at some other duties. Soldiers march better, and fight better, when they hear the music of their band. And-it is so with the boys in school. If a certain lesson, which, under one system of teaching, would be yawned over, and would require an hour's dull work to be learned, can be made an interesting, pleasing occupation, entered upon cheerfully and accomplished energetically and in *half* an hour, time may be saved for other duties, or for play; and not only this, but the *manner* of accomplishing the task will have been such that the mind may have grown vigorous and healthy, instead of idle and morbidly languid.

5th. This is "School *management*."

THE SCHOOL ROOM.

It is very pleasant to go through many of our modern school-rooms and notice the care which has been taken to make everything comfortable and cheerful. The light has been so arranged that the eye is neither dazzled by glare or wearied by gloom: ventilation has been secured in proper kind and degree, so that headache cannot often be complained of there: the desks are adapted in height to the size of the sitter, and the chairs have comfortable backs; pictures are on the walls, an attractive library is accessible, and the polished brass and glass, in the case of apparatus, add to the general effect. Would that *all* school-rooms were comfortable and cheerful! Yet where they are not, much can be done to improve them, and this with but little expense. Even if hard benches and inconvenient desks are the furniture of four bare walls, there may be *something* done to make the place *seem* comfortable and cheerful, if actual improvement is impossible.

Let us suppose the worst case possible—possible, I mean, now-a-days, and try to improve it.

1st. Arrange the desks and seats in some way, so that each pupil can find support for his back and rest for his feet. It need hardly be supposed that this is impossible.

2d. "Tinker" the window-frames, so as to be able to lower the upper sash a few inches. Get calico curtains, if there are no blinds; they will cost about ten cents each.

3d. Cover all holes and ink-spots in the wall with white paper, neatly pasted on; but cover up no dirt which can be washed off. Let the floor be clean and the windows clear.

4th. Tack engravings on the walls, the best you can find; wood-cuts, from newspapers, are better than nothing. Inland boys like ships and steamers, and sea-scenes generally, while boys who live near the coast prefer hunting scenes, and rocks and woods. Maps of the country, the state, the county, town, ward, and block, are desirable.

5th. On the ceiling, draw neatly—in charcoal, if you can do no better—the solar system. Make the sun in red chalk; give the planets their relative size and orbits; let a bushy, red-tailed comet enliven the sketch. On the side wall draw a long black line, five and a-half yards long, to represent a rod; divide the line into yards, one of the yards into feet, and one of the feet into inches. In various spaces, otherwise unoccupied, draw, distinctly, a square yard, a square foot, a cubic foot, an equilateral triangle, and other similar outlines. Let the walls be covered with instruction and amusement for the eye. At first, these figures will attract attention from studies; but in a few days the novelty will have worn off, and although they may attract, they will not distract.

What a change comes over the dreary old room! What a change over the scholars!

Taste, and a little painstaking, can beautify a log-cabin; and if the teacher will exercise these, and if he can also afford money, or get it from the authorities, he may make his rooms seem a second home to his pupils, pleasanter than home, perhaps, to a few. What then? His monthly pay or quarterly income may not be at once increased; but he is adding to his capital, which is reputation and popularity; and if he gains nothing in this respect—which is not justly supposable—he at least gains self-satisfaction and the affection of his scholars, without which there is no pleasure in teaching.

There are many *little* matters which affect the success

of a teacher's daily duties. Is the black-board warped, and cracked and scratched? Take it down, screw a "cleet" on the back, putty up the crack, and paint it black again. There is no expenditure here of anything but a little labor, except for the paint, and that may be made trifling if a few cents' worth of lampblack, a little camphine, a flannel rag and ingenuity are used. Perhaps the chalk is "scratchy." Buy some crayons, if you can; if not, make them. Your boys will help you; and, in a few hours, at an expense of half-a-dollar, you can make enough to last for a whole term, and the improvement will pay you for your trouble.* Have a ledge on the bottom of the black-board, to catch the falling chalk-dust, and to hold "the cleaner." The cleaner may be a stick, two inches square and six or eight long, wrapped around with canton flannel, or plain cotton.

But there is no need of spending more time and space on these things. These improvements on the black-board and its concomitants, may serve as examples of many things in which a little pains may effect much. The teacher must oil the *little* wheels of his machinery, if he would have it all move smoothly.

* *Recipe:* Knead some plaster of Paris with just enough water to make it a stiff paste; roll this on a table; cut it into long strips, four inches wide; with a table-knife divide these into sticks a little larger than your finger; leave them to dry, and *keep* them dry.

ORDER AND METHOD.

Few words are needed under this caption; for order and method are so necessary in a school-room, that there can be but few teachers who have not learned their necessity, and how to secure their good effects. I will only give a few hints which may be of service to some reader.

A clock seems to be an indispensability of a school-room; but if none can be had, the teacher's watch should regulate every exercise. Let every class, or single recitation, have its particular portion of time. Let an order of exercises, or programme, be prepared, a copy of which, written in conspicuous letters, should hang where all can see it. Never let one recitation encroach on the time of another; ask the first question just as the long pointer indicates that the exact time has arrived. Habits of punctuality and promptness are of the utmost importance in school-teaching.

Unless a school is made up of very heterogeneous materials, all, or very nearly all, may be united in some one study. Select the recitation in which the greatest number join, for your first morning recitation, and call the class immediately after opening school. This will require some study out of school, for most of the class, and in this way you may secure such study, if you wish to do so.

It is advised to make the morning session longer

than that of the afternoon, and to occupy it with all the recitations of the mathematics, and with the smaller classes in other studies, so that the afternoons may afford time for the less serious labor, and for general exercises in which all may engage. The last half-hour of the day should be spent in such a way that the close of school shall not seem a release from a prison, as is too often the case. Send them away smiling, in good humour with the school, the teacher, and themselves. If nothing more profitable can be found to be done, tell or read a story. Suggestions concerning various "general exercises" will be given hereafter.

ADMINISTRATION.

I think I hear some teacher-reader say: "*Now* you have reached a subject I am interested in. Arrangements of classes and mending of black-boards are easily enough cared for; but tell me *how to govern my school.* These unruly boys won't *let* me 'make school interesting;' they so try my patience and occupy my time, that I have neither heart nor leisure to attend to minor affairs."

The subject is, indeed, one of the most important which can engage our attention as teachers. It is one which calls for experience and judgment on the part of those who discuss it, and had I only *theories* to offer, or merely *my own* practice to recommend, I should not venture to ask the attention of my fellow-teachers. I am about to submit, in theory and practice, a scheme of school-administration which has the sanction of some of the most experienced and most successful teachers of New England, and I may ask for it the serious attention of my readers.

Principles.

1. Every boy or girl, in schools not "primary," has a *school-conscience*, which decides on all actions contemplated or begun. Every misdemeanor is known as such, and is denounced as such, by this conscience, and no set of rules, however full and explicit, can be presumed to be of any real assistance to it.

Moreover, the child knows full well that the *teacher's* conscience is the same with his own. The boy, about to commit an action, concerning which there has even the least warning been given by his inward monitor, keeps one eye on the teacher, and when he discovers that he is observed, he stops. Good boys rarely look off from their books; bad boys, usually watch the teacher.

One rule only, then, need be made, viz.: "*Do nothing which your school-conscience tells you is wrong.*" This covers the *whole* ground, and no other rule or *furlong* of rules, can.

Of course, this conscience may be depraved, but it is

never entirely seared. It may be educated, and made to appreciate the law. The child's *heart*, too, may be influenced to love the school and the teacher, and it may help the conscience to become strict to warn against actions which are likely to grieve the teacher, or interfere with his wise and kind guidance of the school.

With a belief in the truth of these premises, the teacher must be convinced that it is better to make this "school-conscience," rather than either mere fear or mere love, the moving power of his machine of government.

2. To *govern* as *little*, and *teach* as *much*, as is *possible*, should be the aim of every true teacher.

Is it not true that in many, *too many* schools, there is more of government than of teaching? The attention of the teacher is taken from the class, which may be reciting to him, by a few bad scholars, who, taking advantage of his occupation, are playing at their remote desks; he stops to scold or punish them, and thus neglects his class. Scolding John for making faces makes a decided interference with the teacher's appreciation of the process of a problem in arithmetic or demonstration in geometry. If he can contrive any way by which he may deliver himself from this distraction, he may save time and temper for teaching. In duty to himself and his scholars, he *ought* to contrive or adopt some plan to effect this.

It is claimed that the scheme of silently giving "a mark" for misconduct, as explained, in process and results, below, will enable the teacher to teach more and govern less.

3. The maximum of marks, under this plan, results in expulsion from school. We will suppose that this maximum is ten; that for ten acts of real misconduct on the part of a scholar, as many "black marks" have been publicly accumulating against his name; that, of course, he has known to what result the path of misconduct was leading him; that he has been privately and kindly warned by the teacher; that his parents have been told of his position; that, in spite of all, he has deliberately gone on from the eighth to the ninth, and lastly to the tenth mark, and then has been expelled. Is such expulsion just? Would it have been better to have punished or suspended him? Could he have been reached by any influence?

In answer to the last question, I claim that although some way might have been contrived by which he might have been reclaimed, yet the teacher, with duties owed to every *other* scholar as much as to *this* one, cannot be required or expected to sacrifice their interests to his. All possible *exterior* influences we have supposed exerted for his reformation; and the question becomes, simply, ought the teacher to take time from the good boys and bestow it on this bad one.

Such expulsion *would* be just. The good of the

whole school demands the removal of a scholar who will deliberately expose himself to such a result, in the face of warnings.

The Committee appointed by Congress to attend the recent examination at West Point, use language in their report which bears directly on the subject we are examining. They say that "they are satisfied that 'suspending' or 'turning back' a cadet for excessive demerit, is a pernicious rule for the Academy. If a cadet, with the full knowledge of the penalty attached to excessive demerit, continues to neglect his duty until he exceeds the prescribed limit, he is not only an unworthy subject for the Academy, but his example and influence becomes injurious to others, and he should be dismissed. Suspension and turning are half-way places, into which many are tempted to retreat. The interests of the institution demand summary dismissal."

I admit that it is neither necessary nor wise to make a boys' school as strict in discipline as is the Academy at West Point. There expulsion is not infrequent; in a school it may be very rare. But the *principle* is the same in both, and that is, that there are in *all* societies of men or boys, occasional instances of reckless, obstinate persistence in ill-doing, the relief for which must be the removal of the offender.

I am arguing for the right and justice of removal in certain cases. In reality, however, these cases are of most rare occurrence. In three large schools, conducted under this system, with whose history I have been connected or acquainted for several years, I have known of only three cases of expulsion. A boy who finds himself on the road to disgrace, and approaching the terminus, will strive to turn back, at least at the last turning point. And the system offers him *aid* just at this point, as will be explained below. If he will exert himself in study so much as to attain a high standing for one week, his success may remove one of his "marks;" and, if it be not too late in the term, he may go on and secure the erasure of all or most of them. This is *safe*, for the reason that a boy who studies hard, will have little time for play; and it is *just*, because thus, help is offered to one who wishes to help himself.

4. It is right to take pleasure, and reasonable to take pride in good standing, when it is the result of good conduct.

The man who, by his own exertions, has raised his standing in social life, by labor, either of hands or head, is respected by his fellows, and takes an honest and reasonable pride in his success.

School is a small world. Boys and girls are only little men and women. Some are influenced by a noble regard for the right, and a dislike for the wrong; but these are in minority. A large majority of scholars will be found most easily influenced by appeals to their *pride*.

Such appeals are made, under this system, by means of "the roll," and the published schemes of relative standing. The West Point plan is adopted of making public a list of the scholars' names, arranged in order of merit.

Such are the principles on which a teacher of eminent success, whose memory is cherished by the hundreds who were taught by him, founded this system of school government.

In another chapter will be found some of the "results" of the workings of this plan.

Application of Principles.

At the beginning of establishing this plan I would talk kindly with my pupils, giving them, with illustrations, some of the main points of the foregoing principles. I would tell them that I intended to be a school-teacher, not a school-master. I would make this illustration:—

"Suppose that I am hearing a recitation in arithmetic, and one of the boys is solving and explaining a problem on the black-board. I must watch the process closely to know just what he is doing, to see if he has well learned his lesson, or to help him by some suggestions, if the case is a difficult one. Suppose, now, that while I am thus thoroughly occupied, John Smith, over there in the back seat, seeing that my attention is engaged, takes advantage of it to throw beans at his neighbors. He stops studying himself and prevents others studying. But I happen, just in the very middle of the problem, to see him. Well: I stop the boy at the black-board, make the whole class wait, speak up loudly and crossly (for I am a little vexed) and make the whole school look up from their books, while I scold John, or perhaps call him to my desk to ferule him. John goes back determined to shoot beans as often as he can and dare; we go on with the arithmetic, and in the course of ten minutes, the waters are calm again.

"Now there may be, *very* likely, some other John Smiths in the school. Well; in the course of the day, my attention is taken off from teaching, which is my business, and the whole school taken from studying, which is your business, by some half-dozen such stoppings to scold or punish the John Smiths; we will suppose six times, and six times ten are sixty—sixty minutes lost to all of us by stopping to scold. But besides this stopping, I must be continually on the watch, to prevent mischievousness, and since neither I nor anybody else can do two things well at a time, I must either watch well, and teach poorly, or teach well and let John Smith play as much as he likes. Now there is a fine class in arithmetic, and they have a hard but interesting lesson, and they wanted to hear my explanations, so that those hard sums in to-morrow's lesson might be made easier; but John Smith has cheated them out of them, for almost the whole time of the recitation has been occupied in scolding him, and, as other classes are waiting, they have to go back to their seats uninstructed.

"Now it seems to me, boys, that it is unfair to the arithmetic boys, and unfair to the whole school, that I should devote so much time to scolding and so little to teaching. Besides it makes me cross to scold; I don't like to scold and be cross. If I have to scold and punish often and continually, just think what a life I shall lead, and what an ill-natured old fellow I shall become. *I shall not do so.* If that's what teaching is, I'll give it up and be a blacksmith. No; I have a better plan. You see this roll I have in my hand. I've got all your names written on it in alphabetical order, and opposite the names are little blanks which are to be filled up during the term. Now when I see a boy doing what he and you and I all know to be wrong, I shall not stop to scold, but I shall take down this roll and place a little black mark opposite his name. It will take only a minute, and then I shall go on with my class. Some of the boys, they who are bending over their books, won't know that anything has been going on; no disturbance will have been made, and hardly any time lost. But that boy will know it well; he will see me put down a mark next to somebody's name—for I have noticed that boys in mischief always keep one eye on the teacher ; this is so universally true, that when I see a boy looking at me instead of his books, I always suspect some mischief going on—and as he knows he has been doing wrong, he is pretty sure the mark is for him. At recess, or when school is out, he takes a sly look at the roll and there he sees the mark. If I was mistaken and he was innocent—and this not infrequently happens—he comes to me to inquire about it ; he explains away his mark, and I remove it. But if he is guilty, he takes his sly look, passes on and says nothing ; he knows he deserves it.

"Now when a boy gets *five* of these marks, I take time some afternoon or evening, and call to see his parents. I tell them how he got his marks, and that he knew I would tell them if he received five, but that in spite of my warnings, he went on. I tell them that if he gets five more, I shall ask them to take him away from the school, for I don't want any boys here who will go on deliberately and do wrong ten times, when they know the consequences ; and I add that I shall not take him back again. It seems hard, and perhaps the parents scold about it and say that their son is as good a boy as others ; but I am firm, and refuse to take him back.

"The result is, that the rest of the school sees that 'marks' *mean something*, and they are careful not to get them, careful not to do wrong; and so our school is orderly and you study and I teach.

"Most likely you will all learn the meaning of marks without our having to lose some John Smith. I don't expect to have to send any boy away; I certainly *hope* not to.

"What do you *think* of this plan, boys? Which plan do you like best? the *scolding* plan, or the *marking* plan, (I take a vote.) Be sure you *mean* to adopt it as our plan. If any boy thinks he can't come in under such an arrangement, he had better talk about it to his parents, and get them to send him to some other school. I want to have you all tell them of the plan. It is something new, and they ought to know all about it. Every boy that comes to school to-morrow morning, I shall consider as having made up his own mind, and obtained his parent's consent, to remain under this plan of governing by marks. You may be sure that I have thought carefully of it, and am so sure that it is the best plan, that I shall teach under no other. If my school is small, I shall feel that I had rather teach twenty in this way, than scold fifty or a hundred.

"But there is a way of getting off these marks that you must understand. I will explain it.

"Every boy will have at least three recitations every day. At each of the classes I shall keep a book by me, and if a boy recites well, really *well*, in fact *perfectly*, I shall give him 'four;' if not quite perfectly, 'three;' if only tolerably, 'two;' if badly, 'one;' and if not at all, or absent without excuse, I shall give 'naught.' Now if a boy gets 'four' at each of his three recitations, that will make twelve for the day, and if he does so all the week—five days—he will get five times twelve, which is sixty. Understand; a boy who recites perfectly all the week will get sixty; one who doesn't do quite as well may get fifty or fifty-five, and so the numbers will vary from sixty down to forty, thirty, twenty, and perhaps down to ten.

"Every Saturday I shall add up each boy's numbers for the week, and write the total out, in the blank for that week, opposite his name; so that on Monday morning he may see just how well he stood for the last week. Then at the end of the term I shall add up the total of the weeks. If there are ten weeks, and a boy gets 'four' at every lesson, that is sixty every week, he will get six hundred for his grand total. Some will get this, and the total will vary from the highest number, all the way down to one or two hundred. Then I shall print on a little sheet of paper a list of your names, with the six hundreds at the top, the next highest next, and so on, with the 'dunce' or bad boy, who could study but wouldn't, at the very fag end. These sheets I shall send to your parents, and show them all around town. Who wants to be at the little end! (It may be added to this that a yearly catalogue will be published, in which the names will be arranged in the order of the totals for the terms.)

"Do you understand this system of marking for recitations? Well; if a boy has a bad mark one week, he may get it off by studying hard enough and reciting well enough the next week to get sixty. I do this because I know that if he studies hard enough to do that, he won't have any time to be in mischief, and because I shall see that he is trying to reform himself; and that I always want to encourage.

"Now, boys, you have heard my whole plan of school government. Think of it and talk about it at home, and come to school to-morrow prepared to go to work under it."

Such, fellow-teachers, is the sum and substance of this system. There are NO "rules;" these are not even alluded to; but every scholar understands that he is to obey his own "school-conscience." Of course the teacher will do well to define his own ideas of the behavior appropriate to the school-room, and he may do this without ordaining any other rule than the one given under the subject of "Principles." It has at least the merit of being easily understood and easily applied. It has many others, I think, which will be more obvious when I have spoken of the results. It is based on the principles above-mentioned; if they are just, this system must be.

Results.

1. At the inauguration of such a system, no little trouble may be experienced. Boys who have been accustomed to a scolding or punishment directly upon detection in wrong conduct, as they find that the teacher *does* nothing beyond making a mark against their names, will be apt to think that "marks" are of little consequence, and that they are at liberty to do as they please.

But the teacher will need to say to his school (not individuals) that he fears that on Saturday he shall have quite a number of calls to make. This, in many cases, will produce the desired effect; but he will, for the first two or three weeks, have occasion to see the parents of many of his scholars. He will be glad of these occasions; there will be opportunities for him to explain his system. Of course he will tell them that no very serious misconduct has occurred, and that if they will aid him with their influence, none need be apprehended. In all probability, marks will decrease after these visits. In some cases they may run up to seven, eight, or nine, but he can control the matter then by speaking very kindly but as firmly to individuals, and perhaps to their parents again.

He will find that the appearance of the roll on the first Monday morning will aid him essentially. The idle and mischievous boys of course stand lowest;

they see their positions; and especially if a scheme is prepared of their relative standing, and they find themselves near the bottom of the list, they will be prompted to study harder, and thus will be too much occupied to be in mischief.

The teacher will do well also to bring in as many "general exercises" as possible, to fill up time. He will also commence his plans of out-door amusement, and show himself in these, and in every way, disposed to make school pleasant, so that all shall fear to be sent away. If he has commenced the formation of a company, he may say that *only* school-boys can belong; that if a boy is sent away from school, he cannot remain in the company. By these means it will be strange if he does not succeed in establishing the system and when it *is* firmly established he will have little trouble in carrying it on.

2. The teacher may meet with opposition from parents. Let him have called on all who are likely to feel the halter draw, and so have a poor opinion of the law, before trouble comes on. He will find parents willing listeners, and if he states the case fully and fairly, he will undoubtedly convince them of the excellence of the plan. If any are opposed, talk over the plan very carefully, compare the old and new systems, quote authority, do everything possible to convince, and then if they oppose, advise them to remove their children and keep them away until they can see the-

effects of the plan. Removals will be very few, for the boys themselves will wish to remain. The teacher *may* lose a few scholars at first, and some *may* be sent away, but, *in the end*, he will have no occasion to regret the adoption of the plan. In recent experience I have met opposition from influential sources, but I have built up a school larger and more profitable than any previous school in that city; and I may challenge comparisons in respect to orderly behaviour with any school in the land. This result was the more gratifying for the reason that I began with most unpromising materials.

3. The scholars will certainly approve the plan. Children weary of continual reproof. Besides this, they see the *workings of a plan*, and influences can easily be brought to bear to make them understand that their individual coöperation is necessary; and they will be pleased to aid in making "*our* school" a good one and a pleasant one. Throwing the government of the school on their shoulders, making them *control themselves* under the plan which applies to all, and of which the teacher does little more than register the results—this will interest them. I speak from experience.

4. To sum up the results, the teacher will find that he has *more time to teach, better nature to teach with, fewer cases of discipline, and more complete success*, than he could have under "the scolding plan."

Whispering.

A shoal over which I wish to place a buoy, to prevent running a-ground while sailing under these orders, is—*Communicating in studying hours.* How much trouble has this matter given teachers!

It may be set down as a truth that communication cannot be *entirely* prevented. Even the best scholars will occasionally whisper. They do not intend to violate law, but they "can't help it."

It becomes a question, then. How can we prevent it as much as possible? I answer:

1. By convincing the scholars of the injurious effects of communication on themselves, individually, and on the whole school. This may be done by frankly reviewing, with them, the results of allowing free communication, and discussing plans for avoiding such results. They can be made to understand how that whispering, by leading to talking, and that to playing, is at the foundation of general disorder, by a story like this:

"Holland, you know, is a very low and flat country. Much of it is below the level of the sea. Were it not for the extensive embankments which have been built by that industrious people to keep out the sea, the whole country would be only a vast salt marsh. Instead of roads they have canals. These are very easily built, and are supplied with water from the sea, which is let in through great wooden gates, built in the embankments. In spite of all their care, inundations sometimes happen, which do immense damage. When the tide is high, the water dashes against these sand-banks; and although at first only a little breach is made, yet the loose sand gives way by degrees, until, occasionally, it works a passage, and pours in with resistless fury, washing everything before it—houses, cattle, people and all. They prevent such deplorable accidents only by great care in watching for the first appearance of a break, and immediately stopping it up.

"One night, a little Hollander, about six years old, was coming home very late. He had been away for the doctor, for his mother was sick. As he was passing along near one of the embankments, he heard the trickling of water. It was so dark that he had to hunt around for some time before he found it, but at last he discovered that between the side of one of the gates and the bank, there was a little hole worn, through which the water was trickling in quite a stream. He was a little fellow, but he was wise enough to know that if the water was left to run long, it might soon wear a larger hole, and very likely burst through in a regular inundation before morning. He tried to stop the hole with sand and little sticks, but the water still trickled through; he couldn't find anything, in the dark, which would stop it; so what did he do? He thrust in his little fist, and that stopped the water effectually.

"But after awhile he began to grow sleepy and chilly. He wanted to take his hand out, for his arm ached, and he thought of home and his warm bed. But, like a little hero as he was, he stood to his post. His head nodded, and he almost got to sleep; but the thought that he was saving so much danger and trouble to his own family and the whole village, and perhaps the whole country, gave him strength, and he stood to his post!

"In the morning, very early, his friends and neighbors, who had started out to look for him, found him nodding and shivering at the gate, but still at his post. You may well believe that they were delighted with the prudence and bravery of the little fellow. And it was not long before the whole country heard of it, even the king himself, who ordered a monument to be erected to his honor, and, on the top of it, a marble statue of the little hero.

"Now, boys, let's find the *moral* of this good story. The inundation of disorder in a school generally trickles through a little *whispering hole* that each of you have, just under your noses. And that boy who really wishes to do his part in preventing the pouring in of a whole sea of talking and laughing and playing, will do his best to stop up the whispering hole. In other schools that you have been at, haven't you observed that if the boys were allowed to whisper as much as they pleased, they generally went farther, and became very disorderly? Now, I know that it is rather hard *not* to whisper, if you have been in the habit of it, but are you not willing to try to abstain? Very soon you will get *used* to being silent, and it will be *easy* to do so; you won't think of it at all.

"Boys, you know that I am something of a boy myself. I like play about as well as any of you, and I *believe* in playing, and playing *hard*, and having real '*fun*,' but only in *play-hours*. Just *think* a moment. You play until nine o'clock, and then for only an hour and a-half—only ninety little minutes, you are in school; then comes a recess, full of play; then another ninety minutes, and a noon-time, for play; and it's just so in the afternoon. Now am I not *reasonable* in asking you to abstain from whispering—which *leads to* playing—for only an hour and a-half at a time? Am I not *reasonable?*"

A talk like that will convince a large majority. For the remainder we must have

2. Some arrangement like that of short recesses of five minutes, every half hour, for whispering, without leaving seats, or, at least, forms. Get all to agree to this, to promise on their honor, not to whisper during study hours, if you will give them these recesses. But you must control stubborn cases by

3. *Marking* for whispering, on the ground that al-

though whispering, *in itself*, is not a great offence, yet because it *leads* to worse conduct, because almost all wish to join with you in breaking up the habit, and because the short recesses afford all necessary time for it, it must be regarded as a markable offence.

I have in this way procured a state of things in my school which was gratifying and a source of pride.

REPUBLICANISM.

Under the system which has been advocated there is, perhaps, as *little* of the *form* of government as is possible; but the spirit in which this little is to be administered may be either monarchical or republican, or, better, it may be a happy admixture of both.

The teacher may well be both king and president. There are occasions when he must exercise his autocratic powers, and there are others where it will be wise for him to allow Republicanism to have power.

We will suppose a few instances, for illustration.

1. A boy has committed an offence for which he has been marked. He comes to the teacher with the excuse, "I didn't know it was wrong;" in other words, he declares that his inward monitor did not tell him that the act was wrong.

It is now for the teacher to decide on the probability of the truth of this excuse. If he believes the boy to be dishonest, he may use his authority, as king, and refuse to remove the mark, explaining his course to the boy, or not, as seems best. But if he is in doubt in regard to the boy's honesty : if it is quite possible, owing to the nature of the offence, that he did not know that he was doing wrong; then I would advise an appeal to the school.

After stating the whole case clearly to them, let them vote on the question,—Shall the mark be removed. Do not fail to urge on all the justice of closing the door of sympathy. Tell them that this a question not of mercy but justice. Require a decided majority one way or the other.

Even if, through sympathy, the vote may be to remove the mark, you will lose nothing, for if you fear to trust them, you may, hereafter, remain the king. But you will gain, in either event, the confidence of your scholars. They will see that you are to treat them as beings capable of judging, to some extent, between right and wrong ; you have entrusted to them the power of deciding, and thus have given them the privilege of self-government. If, as is most probable, they have decided the case in accordance with your "instructions to the jury," you have established a rule, applicable to this and other similar cases.

2. Suppose that it is of little consequence at what time your recesses come. Let them decide, by voting, on the times, and, perhaps, on the length of recesses.

3. Suppose that it is a part of your plan to have

school officers,—such as secretary, postmaster, banker, editors, captains "in spelling matches," examiners of writings (to detect errors), in short, occupants of any post of honor. Let these be elected.

In these elections, balloting is generally the best way.

There are other ways by which the Republican element may enter into a system of school government, and I advise its entrance to as great an extent as is possible.

LECTURES.

Lecturing seems to have become an established "institution" among us. We like to sit in a comfortable room, surrounded by our friends and neighbors, and have information poured into us by travellers and essayists, politicians, poets and priests. It is a lazy way of learning, however, and by no means to be recommended as the *only* method of acquiring knowledge; but it has its advantages. If our lecturers would seek to instruct rather than to entertain, we should learn more, though we might laugh less.

Lectures for *children* may be made very profitable to them. They are hungry for information, absorpent of facts, and may be as much pleased with a talk on zoölogy, or the making of cutlery, including jack-knives, as with the exhibition of Signor Blitz, and his learned canaries.

Last winter, the following course of lectures was given in the school-room of the writer:

One of the clergymen of the city—an accomplished scholar—lectured on *Astronomy*. In his lecture, he endeavored to make plain, to youthful understandings, the *causes of night and day*, *of the seasons*, *of eclipses*, and *of the tides*. He talked learnedly, yet clearly, of *the moon*, and exhibited the various theories concerning *aerolites*. He did not overwhelm his audience with the full grandeur of the subject, but picked out the parts most likely to interest and profit children.

A physician talked, on another evening, on *Physiology*. He made the subject *practical*, teaching his audience the advantages of "*sitting up straight*," of *eating slowly*, of *breathing pure air*, of *developing the chest and lungs*. His lecture was eminently instructive and useful.

A railroad engineer came next, who lectured on *Railroads and Locomotives*. He explained the *principles and processes of road-making*, including *bridge-making*, in which part he narrated the wonderful *construction of the Suspension Bridge at Niagara Falls*. He gave us *the history of the locomotive*, *the improvements of various inventors, and the construction and action of locomotive engines*. His lecture was illustrated by drawings and black-board sketches, and was extremely interesting.

A fourth lecture was upon *Electricity*, given by the

writer, assisted by a brother-teacher of the city. Our apparatus comprised (when united) almost everything manufactured by Chamberlain, of Boston, and our experiments were full and successful. One of us did the talking, the other the experimenting, and the boys and their friends were instructed and delighted.

A gentleman of remarkable mechanical abilities, the inventor of several useful machines and applications, consented to give the fifth lecture, on *Machinery*, especially *the operations of all kinds of steam-engines.* Experiments were made illustrating the *properties and powers of steam; the history of steam and its application to machinery*, were very thoroughly given, and the lecture was a decided success. An attractive feature of the entertainment was a *working model of a steam-boat-engine*, and the *high-pressure engine* of a *flouring-mill.*

The illness of a lawyer prevented his delivering a lecture on *Laws and their operations.* He intended to read and explain *the Constitution of the United States*, and of *our own State*, our *laws* and *penalties*, the *modus operandi of elections*, and *the details of municipal government.* His inability to give this lecture was much regretted.

These lectures, together with others given by the writer, on various subjects, occupied nearly the whole of the winter. They were attended by my boys, and many of their parents, sisters, and other friends, and were listened to with the greatest interest. They gave *character* to the school; they evinced the endeavors of the teacher to make his school the best he could. Looking at the matter pecuniarily, it was a wise "move." Two of these lecturers were paid, and paid well, but the money was a profitable investment, as the continued increase of the school testified.

Now, there are many teachers who can get up a course of lectures similar to these, and it would seem that they should need only a hint, to do it; but there are also many teachers who prefer to enjoy their evenings in their rooms, or in society. Let them. If they have any *business-wisdom*, or any benevolent desire to benefit their pupils, or any wish to be popular, they will take this hint, and some of the others contained in this book, and profit by them. If the writer has had any success as a teacher, success both in imparting knowledge and receiving a good income from the business, it has been owing, in part, at least, to his constant efforts to "make school interesting," by such means as he describes in this volume.

A word--and one which may seem almost unnecessary—on the character of these lectures. Their aim should be not to make children *wonder*, but to *inform* and *entertain* them. Scientific words and technical expressions should be avoided; explanations should be made most clearly, and questions encouraged and patiently answered; illustrations should be given, by apparatus and models, as far as practicable, and by drawings, freely and fully. A scientific lecture *can* be made more interesting to children than a story. Whoever has read "The Chemistry of a Candle," or "The Chemistry of a Tea-kettle," in Dickens's "Household Words," will testify, I am sure, to the truth of this assertion. Children are so fond of hearing about the phenomena of nature, the wonders of science, the adventures of travellers, the biographies of eminent men, and similar matters, and they receive so much profit from hearing them, that, for one, the writer takes pleasure in talking to them. The up-turned faces and sparkling eyes of boys and girls inspire me, and I wish to become better qualified to please and profit them.

I subjoin a list of subjects for lectures and talks:

Air.
Electricity.
Railroads and Locomotives.
Travels.
Physiology.
Life at Sea.
Cotton.
Laws.
The Indians.
Physical Geography.
Pneumatics.
Glass.
Printing and Book-making.
Gas.
Chemistry.
Photography.
Geology.
The Metals.
What we eat and drink.
India-rubber.
What we wear.
Elections.

The Steam-engine.
Machinery.
Architecture.
Philology.
Technology.
Gold and Silver.
Fire-arms.
Cutlery.
Heat.
London.
Paris.
New York.
Water.
The Telegraph.
Astronomy.
General History.
Biography.
Ships and Steamers.
Iron.
Painting and Sculpture.
Zoölogy.
Italy.
The Revolution.
Nineveh.
Artificial Teeth.
Japan.
Central America.
Arctic Explorations.
Islands.
The Bible.
Hunting and Fishing.
California.
Australia.
Engraving.
Volcanoes.
The Trades.
Underground.
Whaling.
Politics.
Boys.

There are many books which may be consulted, in preparing for these lectures, a partial list of which will be found at the end of the book. There is one, however, a recent publication, which deserves mention particularly, on account of its usefulness in its department. I refer to *Porter's Chemistry*, a work just issued [1856] by Messrs. A. S. Barnes & Co. One peculiarity and excellence of this book consists in the simplicity of its experiments. A teacher who has no experience in the manipulations of experiments, may venture, with this guide, and at the most trifling expense, to illustrate all the facts and principles of chemistry. Its excellence, also, for a class text-book is so great that there can be no doubt of its very general adoption.

FACTS.

I was troubled, some time since, by the want of punctuality in my scholars. I had just undertaken the management of a school which had "run down," under the control of a man who had governed, at times with severity, at times with laxity of discipline, and I was at a loss what course to pursue to create a reformation in this particular. Acting, however, on the principle of attracting rather than coercing, I determined on the following plan: I was not sure of its success, and I did not make known my motive, intending to try other means if this failed. At ten minutes before nine, I rang the "first bell;" at two minutes before nine, I tolled the "second bell," and at nine, *precisely*, I closed *and locked* the door. After opening school with the usual devotional exercises, I told the few who were at their seats that I intended to spend a quarter of an hour, every morning, in telling them something interesting, something which they would be pleased and profited to hear; and I began at once to tell them about what I saw when I was at Vesuvius and Pompeii. I made the narration as interesting as I could, and, at the end of the fifteen minutes, I opened the door and admitted the outsiders. They had arrived, and had been surprised to find the door locked; a few of them had made a little disturbance, and two or three had gone away; but I said nothing, and we went on with the regular exercises. The process was repeated every morning. I took pains to have something really interesting, and I soon began to observe the effects. They who had heard the "facts," as I called them, told their tardy companions what pleasant information the teacher had given them, and advised them to come in time, if they wanted to hear something nice. I was walking behind two of my boys, one morning, on my way to school—two of the quondam tardies—and overheard one of them say, "Hurry up, or we shan't be in time for the 'fact!'" In a few weeks I had induced a good degree of punctuality, although there were some who could only be persuaded to be punctual by being deprived of their recesses.

In this way I was led to adopt the general plan of giving a fact every morning, a plan which I have retained, and shall continue. There are thousands of facts to be met with, and if the teacher enters in his memorandum-book such items as he cannot fail to meet with in his readings of books and papers, he will gather a large stock of the kind he will need. Some of mine are as follows :

A telegraphic message, sent from New York to St. Louis, will get there about an hour before it started. Why ?

If an ignorant boy were to dispute your assertion that the earth is round, how could you prove it to him. I give the proof, using the black-board as an assistant.

Personal adventures in the Mammoth Cave of Kentucky.

How the English and French, with the Turks, got to fighting with Russia.

About St. Peter's Cathedral, at Rome.

Dr. Franklin, as Postmaster-General.

About corks and sponges.

Mummies.

How they prepare tea in China.

It would be easy to extend the list, but here are enough for a start.

Sometimes, instead of a fact, I read something from Harper, or " Household Words," from the daily paper or a book.

Thus, in the course of a year, what a store of infor mation a boy may gain. If each one enters the fact of the morning in a blank-book, he will make a volume worth a great deal to himself and his friends.

ELECTIONS AND BUSINESS MEETINGS.

Many a young man, on entering the arena of public life, finds himself obliged to take the position of a looker-on, because he lacks confidence to stand up as a contestant, and is ignorant of the rules and customs of the strife. At political meetings, so many of which, of various kinds, are constantly being held in every city and village of the land, at debating clubs, at social discussions, before any audience, however small, the young man who has enjoyed no advantages of training, must sit in a corner, must hide his light, if he has one, under a bushel. He may have clear conceptions of the subject under discussion ; he may, unconsciously, possess no small degree of eloquence ; but timidity, and ignorance of "parliamentary rules," restrain him, and he is eclipsed by some shallow-brain who has learned the art of letting out freely his watery flow of weak ideas. The shallow-brain gets, ultimately, to Congress ; while he of the corner, either afraid or unwilling to "cope with so formidable an adversary," remains in obscurity. It often happens that the civil affairs of a town are managed entirely by a few talkative and ambitious men, who have the gift of gab, and no other gift. To these the wiser men, the men who talk less and think more, submit ; they are out-talked at town-meeting, and because the rabble, who are influenced more by speeches than reasons, vote with the speech-makers, the wiser men are out-voted also.

In advocating early and thorough instruction in debate, for our boys and young men, I may claim, I think, that I advocate the *public* good, as well as their own; for although some boys may be encouraged and aided to become mere speakers, and, perhaps, mere demagogues, not a few will be prepared to meet and combat successfully the errors of vapid fluency.

Boys are fond of imitating men in every respect. They like to hold meetings, in the school-room, for discussion; and if decisions, of greater or less importance, result from discussion, they yield to the majority "like men." The teacher will find no difficulty in initiating and continuing business meetings and debates. There will be, or may be, frequent elections in school. The officers of the company, if there is one, are mostly elective; the officers of the debating club, the postmaster, and banker, may be elected; a school secretary, monitors, if any are employed, leaders in spelling-matches, superintendents of various departments, and other office-holders, may wisely be chosen by the school. There are also frequent questions arising, in which the boys should have a voice. The uniform of the company may be left, partly, at least, to their decision; the arrangement of recesses, perhaps even of the hours of study and recitation, the times and places of parade or of public exhibitions, and other matters of not really vital importance, may safely be entrusted to them for decision. The teacher should seek occasions for calling school-meetings, for the sake of teaching the boys how to discuss and decide.

It becomes a delicate question, how far a teacner may safely leave decisions on school matters in the hands of his scholars. If he is sure of a correct public sentiment among them, and if he is sure of possessing the proper amount and kind of influence over them, he may leave much in their hands. A school cannot be a pure republic; the teacher must be in some, if not most respects, an absolute monarch; and his subjects should be well aware of this power, and of the reasons —which they can easily be made to understand—for maintaining it; but he may yet be partly a President, and with tact, and an uncontrolled veto power, he may govern with safety and success. In my own experience, I have found that the more republican I allowed my school to become, the more pleasantly and easily I could govern it. The very fact that a decision is in their hands, leads them to think seriously on the matter; and it may be safely said that more honest, if not wiser votes will be given by boys, on any given question, than by the same number of men.

We may illustrate this, and, in doing so, I shall draw on actual experience.

In the scheme of administration, in a preceding chapter, it will be remembered that rules, applying to all cases of misconduct possibly to be anticipated, were argued against; the single rule—Do right, and avoid wrong, being the only one considered necessary. Under this rule, James and John failed to come in at the close of recess; they stayed out several minutes after the others came in; and to punish them, and secure greater promptness in them and others in the future, I deprived them of recess for two days. They protested against this, not by words, but by sullen looks and careless actions. On asking them why they were angry at their punishment, they replied that they did not know that I was particular about coming in promptly; that I "had not *said* anything about it;" that they didn't know they were doing anything wrong. I thought this a good occasion for discussing this and similar cases which might occur; so I said nothing in reply to them, but, at the close of school, summoned a school meeting. After laying the case fully before the boys, and giving the reasons of my punishment, I claimed the right to settle the matter according to my own opinions of right and wrong; I appealed to them to decide whether I did not always act fairly, whether I ever showed partiality; "but," said I, "I am willing to leave this case in your hands. The question to be discussed and decided is: Was the punishment just?" My boys had not at that time become accustomed to express their opinions, and no one said anything; so, to start them, I said: "Does no one think that the boys' excuse is a good one, or that cases may not sometimes occur in which there may be doubt whether an action is right or wrong?" This gave material to one of the older boys, who was naturally fond of opposing, and he rose and gave expression to doubts whether a boy could always do right without the guidance of rules. Another boy, a bright little fellow, followed him, who remarked that the question was whether, in this particular case, the punishment was just, and, for his part, he thought it was. At this juncture I urged on them free expression of sentiment, but took no notice of what had been said. A third speaker suggested that the boys were afraid to speak out, lest they might make enemies. I argued against such fear, and obtained a unanimous vote that no one should receive expressions of ill-will for opinions, on account of words uttered in debate; and I succeeded in creating a very general sentiment against gagging free speech. The debate proceeded, and nearly all thought the punishment just. On a vote to sustain my decision, there were but two "noes."

But suppose the case had gone against me; admit that to a certain extent I should lose *prestige* and power; admit that there would be danger, that occasions would be sought to overthrow my authority, and admit that I have not strength and tact enough to weather the storm of rebellion which might arise; *this* at least must be confessed, that the *discussion*, as such, was of great benefit to the boys. The teacher must judge of the safety to his throne of allowing such disputes; but I am of the opinion that if he fortifies his position by acts of kindness, by *thoughts*, rather, and looks, and smiles of kindness, by fairness always, and firmness when necessary, he may trust his boys with considerable power.

The discussion above mentioned led to another, namely: Is it best to adopt a code of laws? This debate was held one evening, and some of the parents attended. To ensure speaking, I privately instructed one of my older boys, one whom I knew I could trust, with arguments in the affirmative: he knew my motives, and was willing to assist me. He was of service in keeping up the debate, which might otherwise have flagged. At the commencement of the discussion I announced my monarchical properties, my possession of the veto, but said that I would yield to a two-thirds vote against me; that if as many as that desired rules, I would yield. I also claimed the right to participate in the debate.

Not to make too long a story, I will say only that we had a most interesting debate, and that, by rather more than a two-thirds vote, it was decided to have rules. A committee was chosen to draw up rules for my approval, and I retained, of course, the right of adding any rules of my own. The result was, that at a second meeting to hear the report of the committee, some fifty rules were proposed. "Oh!" said one little fellow, "I never can remember all those." Others shared his feelings ; a vote to reconsider was passed, and after a renewed discussion and another advocacy of my opinions, the decision of the previous meeting was reversed, and we returned to our old and single rule.

There happened not a few occasions where I allowed power to pass from me to them ; but they never abused my confidence, nor was my authority weakened.

Now, I submit, there can be no question that these debates were of very great service to the boys. They learned how to rise without confusion, "to think on their legs," and to speak without stammering. They learned, also, "Parliamentary rules," and appreciated the courtesies of debate. A debating club was proposed, organized, and carried into very successful operation. Thus, public speaking became popular, and my boys astonished their friends, who came to hear them. If any of them shall attain to eminence in affairs of state, I shall congratulate myself on having been instrumental in preparing them for success, and they may thank me for my efforts in their behalf.

There was no need, in the school of which I have been speaking, of exercises in "declamation." I must admit that I dislike the plan of forcing lads to declaim. I never could see any good results coming, or likely to come, from it. Certainly if boys can be induced to rise and speak *ex tempore*, this is better than the declamation of borrowed language. In the latter case, the boy knows that he is acting a farce ; he does not understand the eloquence of Webster ; he knows that he is on stilts ; but, in the former, he speaks his own thoughts, on a subject in which he is interested, and he speaks freely, naturally, well.

Let me, then, urge on teachers the advantages of encouraging public meetings for discussion or election. On frequent, and even on slight occasions, call business meetings ; or let a written request, signed by a certain number of the boys themselves, be understood as authority for a call.

At these meetings take great care that everything shall be done in accordance with the rules and customs of men.

Let there be a "School Secretary," whose business it shall be to keep accurate records of all votes and resolutions, and to commit to writing a history of all the prominent events of school life. This office should be one of great honor.

At first the boys will be "backward about coming forward ;" this must be met adroitly by the teacher. Let him not refer to the difficulty of standing before an audience to speak, but let him rather urge them to express their opinions as a thing of course, as a necessary step towards a full understanding of the matter in hand. Conceal the fact from them that they are actually "speaking," and they will become speakers without being aware of it.

The teacher must not expect that his business meetings will be as orderly, at first, as those of men; but he should expect to secure good order ultimately. It may be long before they learn Parliamentary rules, and acquire the self-control necessary during the excitement of debate. There will be, at first, much talking and playing among the smaller boys and those not particularly interested: they who are engaged in the contest will be claiming "the floor" often, and several at once; they will be inclined to indulge in personalities, will speak too loud, make assertions instead of arguments, "beg the question," and be variously and frequently "out of order." All this must be patiently and skilfully met and controlled by the teacher; they will improve; boys are plastic in the hands of a man who has their affection, confidence and respect. A simple plan of quieting disorder and repressing excitement, is to stop all procedings and keep the room still for two or three minutes. A few remarks like these will accomplish much: "Boys! I suppose you are anxious to have this question settled. Some of you, also, wish the meeting over, that you may get out to play. Well; to effect both of these objects, I shall suspend operations until the room is quiet, and as soon as you are all still, we will go on and finish our business, come to a decision and close the meeting.

But as soon as you begin to be noisy again, I shall stop the debate again."

The teacher ought generally to preside at all meetings; he alone can control and guide them best; but to give the boys opportunity to learn to act as moderators or chairmen, he should occasionally call on them to preside. If he stands by and supports the officer by his authority, in case of necessity, no trouble can ensue. In a debating club, the boys should have their own officers; but it will be well for the teacher to be present at the meetings as often as he can. He should also take care that they do not select improper or unprofitable subjects for debate.

In concluding this subject, I must express the hope that it will attract the attention of teachers, and that it may lead them to adopt some of its suggestions. I have seen the good effects of the carrying out of these and similar plans for educing colloquial powers, and am satisfied that much good can be done in this department of teaching.

MOOT COURTS.

Moot Courts afford profitable employment for boys' evenings. Information is acquired concerning the forms and technicalities of that mystery, "the law," of which most men are ignorant. There is no reason why boys may not be taught to understand, perfectly, the whole process of a suit at law, whether criminal or civil. In addition to this, opportunities are offered for practice in this kind of public speaking. As has been remarked in the preceding chapter, boys will learn to speak fluently on subjects in which they are interested, when they will continue mere awkward declaimers of the eloquence of Webster or Burke. If the case to be tried is one which will amuse, excite, or in any way interest the school, the counsel on either side will enter into the trial most heartily, and the kind of practice they will have will be of service to them.

To accomplish anything by Moot Courts, the teacher must be sure to lay his plans in such a way that the first one shall be a success. The case must be one of no great difficulty; and it is suggested that a criminal would be better than a civil case; but it must present such features that the counsels for plaintiff and defendant, or State and prisoner, may each have grounds for argument. It is advised that the teacher examine the records of remarkable trials, and, from two or three of the best of them, select materials to make up a case of the right kind. Or, one of the school-boys may be arraigned on a charge of arson, or theft, or assault, or trespass.

Take care that the counsel make thorough preparation, that the witnesses understand just what testimony to render, that the sheriff knows his duties, and that all the details of the trial are properly prepared. If a lawyer can be induced to act as judge and guide the trial in proper channels, the success may be made more certain.

After a while, the boys will have learned how to conduct a court, and they may be trusted to carry through the whole business, from a grand jury presentation to a verdict. It will be well to give them the entire management; the teacher, of course, advising, and in reality controlling.

Instances have been known in which a teacher has effected, by means of Moot Courts, the detection and punishment of offenders whom he had been unable to reach by the ordinary forms of school government.

In a certain school, a long series of petty thefts had annoyed the scholars and troubled the teacher. Articles of inconsiderable value had been stolen from desks, such as knives and pencils, books, drawings, &c. The teacher's desk, also, had been more than once pillaged or ransacked. At last the matter became important, by the theft of gold pens from three desks in one week, and the scholars grew clamorous for an investigation. Strange to say, suspicions could be fastened on no one in particular, and the two or three who had been hastily charged with the offence, were most anxious for an opportunity of clearing themselves. The teacher was at a loss what course to pursue, but at length hit upon the expedient of a legal investigation. A grand jury was elected, instructed in their duties, and the case was left in their hands. They acted with the utmost secresy. It was unknown that any steps had been taken. Police-boys were appointed, and the building was watched for several nights, and at last the offender was caught. He had entered the school-room by means of a false key, and was apprehended in the very act of opening a desk.

It is unnecessary to detail the events which followed. Suffice it to say that the offender was tried, most skilfully defended, found guilty, and sentenced to expulsion; with a recommendation to the mercy of the executive,—the teacher.

The defence rested mainly on the good character of the prisoner, who was one of the best scholars and the mildest and most inoffensive boy in school, and on the fact that he was not caught in the act of stealing. But by an incautious admission on the part of the prisoner's counsel, the prosecuting attorney turned the case against the prisoner, and the jury brought in their verdict of guilty. Restitution, however, had been made in full; and it became evident, before the verdict, that the offender was possessed of a mania for appropriating; that he had stolen for the love of the adventure of stealing, had hoarded the articles stolen, and had acted from no malicious or wicked notions whatever. On this account, and because the jury and the sentiment of the whole school was in his favor, pityingly, the recommendation to mercy was added to the verdict.

The prisoner would have confessed to the teacher, on apprehension, but was persuaded to allow the case to come to trial, for the sake of affording the advantages of a thorough trial to the school. Whether this was best or not, may be left to the decision of the reader.

The results of this case were most fortunate. The offender was thoroughly cured of his propensity, and, owing to his evident reformation and his otherwise excellent character, he was allowed to remain in school, and did not suffer from any serious display of ill-feeling from his companions. The benefits derived from the trial were very considerable. Several napkinned talents for public speaking were brought to light and put at interest; and all were profited by becoming thoroughly acquainted with the forms of law.

I have given this trial in detail, partly because the teacher may learn from it one way with which to deal with anomalous cases of discipline, and partly to serve as a model of a "case" for trial. It happened to be one in which school-boys would be interested, and one which offers good material both for the prosecution and the defence. There are two or three strong points to be made on either side, and it cannot be for the lack of material that the trial may not be interesting.

If it shall add to the motives of a teacher for trying the experiment of organizing a Moot Court, I may say that all teachers who have tried, with whom the writer has conversed on the subject, have expressed unqualified approval of the plan, and satisfaction with its results.

SCHOOL POST-OFFICE.

Facility in *expressing* one's thoughts is the next best thing to *having* thoughts worthy of expression. "I *know*, but I cannot *explain* it," is very often the honest excuse of good scholars in the recitation-room. In writing compositions, in the analysis of problems, even in common conversation, many, if not most children, find it difficult to express their thoughts. This difficulty must be met early by the teacher who remembers his duties as an educator, as well as an instructor, and he will adopt various methods to assist his scholars in clothing their thoughts in appropriate language. In his classes, he will encourage clearness in explanation: in arithmetic, for instance, will be better pleased to hear one problem thoroughly analyzed and clearly explained, than to see six of them done on slate or black board.

In my own experience, I have found that general exercises, having for their purpose the educing of thought, are very useful. In various ways I require the frequent use of pen and pencil, and always with good results. I give now one plan, and shall mention others hereafter.

I should say here that the main features of this plan

have been borrowed from an eminent teacher, whose success with it has been greater even than mine. I am also indebted to him for many valuable suggestions.

Preparations.

1. Some contrivance to represent a Post-Office. My own is an oblong, narrow box, resting on its narrower side, on a high table which stands out three feet or more from the wall; its front is a window-sash, its back, two doors, opening at the middle; there are thirty-six "boxes," and the lower middle pane of glass is removed, and replaced by a little door, hinging at the top and fastenable within. The post-master, at office-hours, stands behind the table; the two doors are opened, and shut him off, on the sides, from interference; he opens the front trap-door, and receives and delivers letters. The expense of this, nicely grained and varnished, and provided with lock and key, was ten dollars. No doubt something might be contrived for less; and if expense must be avoided, the post-master may use a table-drawer. Yet the "boxes" and trap-door give character to and add to the success of the plan.

2. Some cards, about half the size of a common visiting card, printed, or, almost as well, written upon

with the numerals expressing the values of all our silver coins, of the regular decimal coinage. The "three-cent-pieces," needed especially at the office, must be more numerous than the other coins, and the teacher will judge from the size of his school, how much money to issue. To prevent counterfeiting (although I have found no need of prevention) the teacher's name may be signed on the back of each card.

Operation.

In announcing the plan to the school, enlarge on the advantages of learning to write letters well; speak of clerks, who, on applying for a situation, are requested to address in their own handwriting; and remark that of two applicants, the one sending in a neatly written and properly spelled and punctuated letter, and the other sending one just the reverse of this, he who writes the better letter will stand the better chance of getting the situation. There are many other things which may be appropriately said, which I need not mention. The teacher then explains the working of the plan from the following:

Harry writes a letter to Charles; it must be a *regular* letter, on at least a half-sheet of common writing paper, inclosed in an envelope, neatly sealed and directed; it must contain at least one page of matter, written on some sensible theme. Harry takes this to the post-office, hands it to the postmaster through the door, and pays a three-cent card for it, as postage, in advance. The postmaster will not receive it if it is badly sealed or improperly addressed, but if it is properly prepared, he places it in Charley's box, and when he applies for it, the postmaster gives it to him. He (Charles) then looks over his letter carefully, and charges Harry one cent (card money) for every mistake, either of spelling or punctuation; and if it is carelessly written, or contains vulgar language, he brings it to the teacher, and he allows a fine of from three to twenty-five cents. Now Charles must write a reply to Harry, within two days, (school days,) and Harry has a chance to charge Charley for his mistakes. Neither will write carelessly, it is to be presumed, for the letter costs three cents to begin with, at the post-office, and if written without care, will cost still more for its errors. If these two boys are equally correct at writing, they will each receive about as much as they pay out, but if one writes worse than the other, he will lose and the other will gain. So it behooves each one to write as carefully as possible, using his Dictionary often, and consulting the teacher if necessary, and to look very closely for mistakes in his replies, so as to lose as little, and gain as much as possible.

Boys have been known to make as much as six, eight, and sometimes ten dollars in a quarter. The writing is to be done out of school, although I sometimes allow *good* scholars to write in school, but these only when I am quite sure that they have learned all their lessons.

I now lend each one a dollar. This they may pay back at the bank as soon as they please, but it *must* be paid at the end of the term. Every dollar above the amount loaned, given in at the end of the term, I redeem by paying —— (say ten or fifteen) cents in silver; but if the boy has lost everything, he must pay me the same on every dollar he has borrowed. He may borrow more at the bank by giving his note, endorsed, for thirty or sixty days, and paying regular bank discount. In some cases I allow the banker to "renew" notes, giving "extension" to some time in next term. I have a set of Rules in accordance with these general principles.

There needs to be a Postmaster. He is to be paid by the rent of his boxes, for which he may charge whatever prices he may think best. If he asks too much, he will not rent many; and if he charges too little, he will not make much money. He will have to open his office twice a day, at the close of school in the morning and afternoon. He had better hire an assistant, for if he is away, and the office is not open at the time, he must pay a fine. It is well to elect the postmaster to serve for one term:—elect by ballot.

I appoint a Banker. He must be one who knows

something about book-keeping, for I require accurate accounts of all money passing through his hands. He must get two boys to be his security for honesty (as the banks all do), and I pay him as salary —— per cent. on the amount of money passing through the bank. Bank must be open once a day, at close of school in the afternoon. Every boy keeps a bank-book, as well as Dr. and Cr. accounts with all his correspondents.

The teacher will take care that all business, either with the post-office or bank, shall be done in accordance with regular business forms. He will reserve to himself the right to decide all disputes concerning errors. He will so arrange the Rules and penalties that charges shall be promptly paid, either in cash, (card-money,) or negotiable paper. If there are no "boxes," he will pay the postmaster a salary, perhaps a per centage on his cash received, and by giving him the franking privilege. The "Rules" must be posted, somewhere, conspicuously.

A better plan, perhaps, than redeeming the money with silver, is one that I have tried: it is to have an auction at the end of the term, at which such things as boys like to possess are purchasable with card-money, and with this only. I sometimes buy articles for the auction from the boys themselves; as, a knife, or a sail-boat, (model) or a book, with the parent's written consent; paying them in card-money. I buy these things, and others, during the term, and when I have acquired anything attractive, I announce it, and perhaps display it, as an incentive to them to try to make money for the auction. The bank may be a bank of deposit, with or without interest to be allowed. The banker should prepare a balance for every week ; and auditors may be appointed.

I give prizes in my school, and have sometimes, at the scholars' request, paid them in card-money. Thus, at the auction, the boy may buy what he chooses ; if a book, I write his name and honor on the fly-leaf. The objection to this plan is, that a boy who has worked hard and successfully in the post-office, may be out-bid by one who has been his inferior in the post-office, but has taken one or more prizes. The objection may be removed by some ingenuity in receiving bids, or by putting up certain articles to be bid for with post-office money, and certain others, as perhaps books, to be bought with prize-money.

He may, wisely, make a rule that letters containing three closely written pages shall be exempt from postage. Replies must be as long as letters received, under penalties for every ten words less.

Results.

1. I have known forty letters to pass through the office in a day, in a school of fifty-five scholars. I have

seen very decided improvement in every respect; indeed, I may say that in many instances I have been unable to detect the least error in long letters. I have received the eulogiums of parents on the plan. I know that it adds to the general interest of my school.

2. The boys learn, practically, the forms of banking and of making notes, for they may be allowed to borrow from each other. The importance of this is unquestionable. If the teacher has a class in bookkeeping, he may require the members of it to act as bankers, each a week in turn.

3. But as a grand result, the boys learn how to express their thoughts; they become accustomed not only to clothe their thoughts with words, but also to clothe them well, and even elegantly.

To sum up all, the beneficial results of this post-office plan are so great that I earnestly advise every teacher who values either the improvement of his scholars, or the advancement of his own reputation as a teacher, to adopt it in this form, or in some other and better one. The money spent will be an addition to his capital, both in his present school and in his general reputation.

THE NEWS.

In a school of the writer's acquaintance, there is a class which is worthy of mention. The elder boys, of whom there are fifteen or twenty, prepare, on Saturday, a digest of the news of the week, which they report on the following Monday. One boy is called upon for the foreign news, another for domestic, a third for political, a fourth for literary, a fifth for local. When any event of unusual importance has taken place, either abroad or at home, this is made the theme of particular examination. This is one of the regular classes of the school; its recitations are "marked" by the same standard with the others. The teacher takes care to create and maintain interest among the members; he makes himself thoroughly acquainted with the news of the day, and, by a few words of geographical, political, or literary explanation, gives significance to facts and rumors, which might otherwise be devoid of attraction, and difficult to be retained in memory.

For the younger members of a school, a plan, carried into successful operation by another teacher, may please the reader. A large scrap-book is prepared, a committee of selection is chosen, a paste-pot made ready, and contributions are invited. Every day there are brought in the clippings and cuttings, of all the boys, from home papers. One brings an anecdote, another an interesting item of news, a third an arithmetical puzzle, a fourth a beautiful or an amusing wood-cut. These are handed to the committee, who decide, by a majority, on their insertion; and they paste accepted articles into the scrap-book. Pictures are almost always acceptable; short stories and interesting facts are plentiful; all are gratified at the growth of the book; and, in a short time, a grand collection is made, and a fund of entertainment and instruction provided. The book is kept on a shelf, similar to those used in reading-rooms, and all enjoy the reading of it. The teacher has now several huge volumes of this kind. One of them was sold at auction, for "post-office money," last term, and brought a high price. I envy the purchaser his possession.

LIBRARY.

A good Library is a very desirable addition to any school. The expense of purchasing books deters teachers from providing them. Let me tell how libraries have been procured, of excellence in size and character, at very little expense to any one, and none at all, to the teacher. After talking up the subject in such a way that interest in the subject is secured, the teacher may invite his boys to lend some of their own books to the school, such books as they would be willing to lend to their companions. These they are to cover firmly, and their names are to be distinctly written within. In a school of fifty, one hundred volumes may easily be collected, perhaps more. These are to be loaned out under strict regulations. Fines are to be collected for neglect to return within specified times, for losses, injuries or defacements, and these fines may be easily collected, if there is the understanding that the money is to be applied to the purchase of new books. Let those who have no books, or are unwilling to expose their treasure to miscellaneous handling, be allowed to become members by the contribution of a certain sum of money. When this original collection becomes stale, invite contributions of money for its increase. Let the teacher head the list of contributions with as liberal an offering as he can afford; let him ask aid from some of his wealthy patrons; his boys will, themselves, contribute dimes and quarters freely; the library may, by these means, be made all that a school can need.

Every teacher should possess encyclopædias or books of reference; these he should leave for access to his school, not to be taken from the rooms, but to be examined and returned to their places.

When a boy leaves school, he may of course, take with him the books he has loaned, and he may also be entitled to select a volume of a value nearly equal to any money he may have contributed. If this is understood by all, contributions may be more liberally made.

It will be well to entrust the care of the library to a librarian chosen from among the scholars. Such posts of trust and honor should be made numerous in a school; boys should early learn to fulfill duties of various kinds, the more the better.

READING ALOUD.

The young gentleman or young lady who can read aloud correctly and gracefully possesses an accomplishment which will enable him, or her, to give much pleasure to others. How pleasant is that family circle, which, in a winter evening, is gathered around the fire, beneath the mellow light of a shaded lamp or "burner." The father, wearied by the labors of the day, enjoys the embracing arms of an easy-chair, and desires no more vigorous occupation than that of a listener. The good mother, ever busy in the service of her children or husband, sits knitting on the opposite side of the hearth. The elder daughters are sewing or crocheting, the children are half-busied with paints or quiet toys, and all are listening to an elder son or brother, who is reading aloud some interesting book of travels, or one of Dickens's stories. He reads in no drawling, sing-song tone, but throws life and character into the language of the author. He delivers the remarks of "Cap'n Cuttle" in a rough, solemn, and oracular voice, or imitates the hopeful tones of "Wal'r's" voice, or the "no-consequence" air of "Mr. Toots." If Stephen's Travels, or Layard's Nineveh, is the book of the evening, he narrates their adventures and discoveries in a manner which would become him were he himself the traveller, telling the story of his own adventures and discoveries. The time passes unobservably, and when nine o'clock comes—the bed-time of the little folks—they beg to sit up a little longer, and are only persuaded to go willingly with the promise that "brother shall read again to-morrow evening."

It is this accomplishment which many desire to see taught in schools. Almost all children *can* be taught to read well. What child is there who cannot *tell* a story well. The boy has met with some tragic or amusing adventure, and he runs in and gives his mother a most glowing description of it; he imitates, unconsciously and naturally, the voices of his playmates who were engaged with him in the affair; he makes present the past event. Now, can it be denied that he may be able to *read* the same, or a similar adventure, with the same tones and emphasis of voice with which he told it? But for so long a time children have been taught to read at school from books which they do not understand, or in which they take no interest, that they have acquired a drawling way, a lifeless, mechanical style, in which to "speak up loudly and distinctly" is excellence enough. I am glad to admit that a reformation has begun in this department of instruction, but there will need a generation or so of school-children, and the constant and varied efforts of teachers and parents, to recover from the effects of the old-fashioned way.

A plan to accomplish something in the way of improvement in school-reading, which has the recommendation of success, and is, at the same time, an interesting exercise for the school, is as follows:

Let the teacher select a story from some book or magazine, which he will be sure shall interest his boys. Let him give the book containing it to some boy, asking him to read the story over to himself a few times, to become familiar with it; and at or near the close of school, let the boy read it aloud to his schoolmates. Before commencing, however, let the teacher recall some amusing event which has recently taken place, or select some anecdote from the scrap-book, and let him repeat this to the school in a slow, drawling way, in a forced, unnatural voice. They will all laugh at such a rendering, and will appreciate the meaning of the teacher when he changes his tone and style, and gives them the event or anecdote in a natural, unaffected way. Turning now, to the reader, let him remark to him, "You can take your choice of these two ways of reading." As he reads, do not discourage him by too frequent interruptions, but, occasionally, when he relapses into the drawl, repeat the passage, kindly, in the better way, and ask him to notice and imitate your manner. When he has ended, read to them yourself, some other good story, and let your style be worthy of imitation. Have these readings often. Be sure that the story is naturally written, is lively or exciting, in short, make the exercise one that all shall be glad to engage in. A good time for the reading may be on Friday afternoon, at the close of school. Hawthorne's "Wonder Book" and "Twice Told Tales," Dana's "Two Years before the Mast," "Chambers' Series," and "Household Words," are books from which good stories may be selected; but, in these days of books, the teacher need seldom be at a loss for a story.

COMPOSITIONS.

One method of making that bugbear of "composition" less frightful, may be grafted upon the above-mentioned reading-exercises. Let the story which has been heard from the teacher or the reader, be the theme for a composition. Require the scholars to write out the story from memory, and say to them, by way of encouragement, "When you get home, and your mother or father asks you what you have done to-day, you will be very apt to speak of having heard this story. They will want to know what the story was, and you will tell them; you won't have any *difficulty* in telling them the whole story clearly. You will not remember the words of the book; you will tell it in your own words. Now this is just the way in which I want to have you *write* the story. Write it just as if you were telling it at home."

They should write it at first on their slates; then

they should look over the work, to correct mistakes, and then copy it into their blank-books.

In this way thoughts are furnished them, and they practice themselves in *giving expression* to these thoughts. This, as I think, is at the foundation of success in composing, namely: *expressing* thoughts, no matter whence they are derived. *After* the student has learned to write out his ideas, and to write them grammatically, and with correctness in punctuation and the other details, he may enter on a course of inventing ideas for himself. If this course is adopted, the writer, when he has learned to express himself freely and correctly, will be no longer impeded, clogged, confused with *how* to write, and the *what* to write will arrange itself clearly and easily in his mind.

Another advantage of this method is, that children are fond of writing stories, while they dread "compositions," and they can thus be induced to get into a *habit* of writing, so that they themselves, unconsciously, strip the object of their fears of its disagreable disguise.

The plan of the writer in teaching this subject has long been founded on these principles, and the successes of the plan have determined its excellence.

In detail, it is as follows:

On Wednesday afternoon a story is read; one-half of the school—say the younger, write this off upon their slates, as roughly as they please, taking care only to get in the whole story, without omissions or alterations; they then write it out fully, and as correctly as they can, on half foolscap sheets of paper, and hand them in to me, at the close of school. I take these exercises, and at my leisure I examine them, and correct them with *red ink*. A mistake which I think they can correct themselves, I merely underline; an error which is correctible in the narrow space between the lines, I correct in writing, but more important errors I leave for verbal explanation; I mark the place with a large interrogation-point, and require them to come to me at my desk to talk about it. On the following Wednesday, these corrected exercises are distributed to them, and they are required to copy them, noting carefully the corrections, into their blank-books. At the same time, I read another story for the other, or elder, half of the school. I give them a longer and more intricate story than I gave to the first division, but the process of writing, correcting and copying is the same.

In "marking" these writings I give a high grade for comprehensiveness, clearness and accuracy, in the exercise; for absolute correctness and good penmanship in the copy.

Occasionally, instead of reading a story, I give to my older division the skeleton of a story, or merely the theme for a narration or description. From their number I select the best to form an advanced class, which I instruct particularly in the art of composing, For this class I would recommend "Brookfield's First Book in Composition" as a valuable text book upon this subject; also, "Parker's Exercises in English Composition," and "Quackenboss' Second Book," on the same subject. Additions are made to this class, frequently, by promotion.

In concluding the subject, I am pleased to be able to say that I rarely fail to make "composition" a pleasant and easy study, and that my scholars succeed in becoming good composers.

SCHOOL PERIODICAL.

To encourage writing and to afford profitable entertainment to his school, the teacher may think it best to establish some kind of periodical. If no better plan occurs to him, he may adopt the following:

Fold a large sheet of printing-paper in newspaper shape; let it be ruled in columns; let editors, chosen by vote of the school, paste into the spaces articles selected from the journals of the week, together with original matter, written on paper which has been cut to fit the spaces; encourage offerings (original) from the scholars by announcing a prize (in post-office money) for the best story, in three chapters, or for the best piece of poetry. With original matter and selections, the editors need never be at a loss to fill their columns. Let the ornamental heading of the first page be an original design and drawing. Advertise for these, offering rewards for the one accepted ; and have a new one for each issue. Let the teacher encourage the enterprise by contributions in the shape of good selections, and of stories written to praise or ridicule some boy's habits. Let the paper remain during the week on a reading-desk, similar to that proposed for the scrap-book, and at the end of that time, be preserved for comparison and future readings.

From this, as a beginning, there *may* grow a periodical worth printing, but the writer's experience has led him to think that the publication of school periodicals, in printed form, "costs more than it comes to."

GEOGRAPHICAL GAME.

About ten years ago the writer attended a Teachers' Institute in Massachusetts, under the direction of Horace Mann. Among the exercises was the following :

The teachers, ladies and gentlemen, arranged themselves on opposite sides of the room, forming, however, a continuous line, standing with their backs against the wall. At the request of Mr. Mann, the gentleman who stood nearest to him repeated the name of a town and gave its State or country. Perhaps it was "Boston, Mass." The final letter of Boston, N, was the initial letter for the next person, who gave, we will suppose, "Newport, R. I." T came to the third in order, who may have given "Trenton, N. J." Thus it went on. "No one may give a town which has been given before," said the director.

The circle, or parallelogram, of teachers was able to preserve its completeness during the first "round," although the last dozen of the hundred and fifty were somewhat puzzled to think of new towns, and others were in momentary difficulty when the letter which came to them was a Y or a K, or a Z. Towns which begin with E also became scarce.

At the conclusion of this round, Mr. Mann remarked that some distinct rules were necessary before entering upon the second round. After saying that towns might be mentioned from any part of the world, he laid down the following rules:

Any one *repeating* a name of a town;

Any one failing to give the State or country to which the town belonged; or

Any one failing to give a correct name, within one minute by the director's watch,

——must sit down.

He remarked, also, that as the victory would belong to the last one standing, it became all to give such names as ended in a difficult letter for his or her successor.

The second round was begun, and now there were droppings away from the hitherto intact rank. It happens that there are many names of places which end in E, and but few, comparatively, which begin with that letter. In addition to this difficulty, by this time they who had not pretty good memories, or an intimate acquaintance with geography, found it hard to think of a name not already mentioned, within the sixty seconds; or they *repeated* a name, and were obliged to sit down. For these reasons, and others, at the end of the second round, one-half of the original number were in their seats. At the end of the third round only ten were left; but these were veterans, who were as familiar with their atlases as their spelling-books. This Spartan band was composed of six ladies and four gentlemen. As the fourth round was commenced, the attention of the wounded was riveted upon the survivors, and the heroes buckled their armor tightly around them and prepared for the contest. To the spectators it seemed as if there were no more towns left; but they were mistaken. The resources of the ten seemed inexhaustible, and they maintained their positions during one more round. At this point the time was lengthened to two minutes; but even with this indulgence, they could not all maintain the floor. Gradually the number was reduced to five, to three, to two; a lady, on one side of the room, and a gentleman on the other. The excitement now approached its climax: it was not only teacher against teacher, but sex against sex; and no one of the ladies wished the gentleman to resign in deference to the laws of gallantry, as he proposed. They began: for some ten minutes they stood firmly; but at last the lady gave her opponent the initial K. It "posed" him; he ransacked his memory in vain for a town beginning with that letter, which had not already been given, and at the expiration of his time he expiringly enunciated "*Kalcutty*," (Calcutta) as a joke, and yielded the palm of victory to the lady. The excitement and enthusiasm now climacterized in a *furor* of applause, from both sides; and, amid expressions of delight with the exercise and its results, the teachers gradually subsided into sufficient calmness to go on with the next subject on the programme.

This exercise was thus illustrated by that excellent teacher, Mr. Mann, that it might recommend itself as an exercise for schools. I suppose that it has been adopted in many Massachusetts schools; but as I have not heard of it elsewhere, I think it worthy of a renewed and more general recommendation.

The teacher who adopts it will be pleased to notice the eagerness with which his scholars, after once learning the *modus operandi*, will examine their maps, to prepare for the next trial; and he will be sure that, in addition to the advantage the exercise gives in inspiring the study of Geography, he has added another to the list of profitable school amusements.

The plan may be varied, by confining the contestants

to particular maps, and by requiring more minute descriptions of the places named; as, for instance, "New Haven, Ct.; situated on Long Island Sound; has about 30,000 inhabitants; is noted for its college—Yale." Or, instead of names of towns, rivers and mountains may be mentioned, without restrictions as to initial letters, but within the rule concerning repetition.

The writer has applied the principle on which this game is conducted in another way. Minuteness of observation, and accurate fullness in description, are desirable acquirements for writers. In my classes in composition, I have sometimes required a division to name the adjectives describing a fountain, a landscape, a storm, an accident; or the events of an excursion, a term at school, a war, a narrative of adventure (as Robinson Crusoe's); and have then required them to write a composition on the theme thus examined.

ARITHMETICAL GAME.

I well remember the interest with which "we boys" used to engage in this game. At a quarter before four o'clock, our teacher would say—"Slates and pencils." In a twinkling we were ready, and, *auribus erectis*, sat waiting for "the sums." He who first solved a problem correctly, and announced the result, was allowed to go; and with what triumphant looks did the victor gather his books and march out from among those who were still "kept in!"

The object of the exercise is to give boys practice in rapid calculation. If the school is one of heterogeneous character, as almost all schools are, it will be necessary to make two or three divisions, in which boys of nearly equal attainments are to be classed. Let each division have opportunity for practise in turn. The teacher is to prepare or select problems of ordinary difficulty, within the capacity of the division. He must be certain that his answers to these are correct. Very slowly and distinctly he announces a problem; the boy who first raises his hand is supposed to have found the answer, and if, on being allowed to state it, he is "right," he is allowed to go; if he is wrong, another one is given. This is continued until all have worked their passage out. Details of arrangement may be left to the reader.

DICTATION EXERCISES.

The importance of the constant use of the pen or pencil, in pursuing many studies, is now generally admitted. Whether to assist in remembering or expressing thought, this agent is most valuable, and children cannot too early become accustomed to its use. Children are fond of using writing-materials, and will often busy themselves most industriously over-an exercise to be written, when they would be idle over a task requiring only abstract thought. They seem to themselves to be accomplishing something, if the results of their labors take form in black and white. For instance, they may be led to take pleasure in preparing their lessons in Geography in the form of statistical tables, and the facts and events thus arranged would be impressed, by sight, upon their memories, while, if they were to study the lesson in the ordinary way, they might labor without spirit, and with unsatisfactory results.

It is recommended that the teacher seek various and numerous methods of giving employment to the pencils of his scholars. There is an excellent little book which will aid him in doing this, called " Northend's Dictation Exercises :" it costs but little, and is worth much. It is the result of wise experience, and contains many most valuable suggestions.

I will not quote from it, but rather urge teachers to buy it, and will venture to give here a few additional hints.

In spelling, the writing out of words in distinct form aids the memory wonderfully. Let the teacher dictate the words which he wishes learned, making such classifications of them, at different times, as he thinks best, and require his scholars to write them distinctly on their slates ; let him give them time to make these as correct as reference to the dictionary and applications of rules can enable them to do, and, at the end of a certain time, let him send "examiners" to look over the slates. These "examiners" may be, at first, boys who are of high standing in this department; they are to hold office, however, only as long as they make no mistake themselves. If one of them overlooks an error (left, perhaps, on purpose to catch him), or reports as an error a word, or words, which the examined finds, by reference to the dictionary or the teacher, to be rightly spelled, the examiner must be deposed, and the boy whom he has corrected may take his place, to hold office on the same tenure. The examiners are to report errors to the teacher, and a certain number may lower the standing of the errorist. Examiners are anxious to retain an honorable office, and they scrutinize, most critically, the exercises of their fellows; these, in turn, are desirous of ousting and supplanting the examiners, and, at the same time, are careful not to lower their standing by being reported as having made mistakes. This plan has worked most admirably.

With the same system of "examiners," various grammatical exercises may be given; such as writing sentences, and denoting the several parts of speech by abreviations, as *n.* written over a noun, *adj.* over an adjective, *adv.* over an adverb, &c. There are various other ways of employing these means in studying Grammar, but it will be needless to enumerate them for any inventive teacher.

Reference has already been made to a method of studying Geography with the fingers as well as the eyes.

In Arithmetic, younger classes may profitably employ themselves in copying the muliplication table, and the tables of weights and measures.

I have been very much pleased with exercises in defining, conducted on the following plan, for which I am indebted to Mr. Northend, and which I cannot forbear quoting : I have offered prizes, of inconsiderable value, or "credits," (or "plus-es") in standing, for the six longest, fullest, clearest and most correctly written definitions of twenty such words as these: cotton, gunpowder, sugar, steel, animalculæ, gold, &c. I have received, often, from six to twelve closely written foolscap pages of definitions on twenty such words, and could see that the writers had examined every encyclopedia or book of reference within their reach. These exercises were written out of school.

It will not be difficult for the teacher to add to this list many other and better exercises.

10*

LIST OF BOOKS

FOR A TEACHER'S LIBRARY.

THE TEACHER'S LIBRARY, in 7 vols. (A. S. Barnes & Co. Publishers.)
BARNARD'S AMERICAN JOURNAL OF EDUCATION.
" SCHOOL ARCHITECTURE.
" LECTURES AND PROCEEDINGS OF THE AMERICAN INSTITUTE OF INSTRUCTION.
" NATIONAL EDUCATION IN EUROPE.
" NORMAL SCHOOLS.
THE SCHOOL AND SCHOOL-MASTER, by BISHOP POTTER and G. B. EMERSON.
TEACHING A SCIENCE, THE TEACHER AN ARTIST, by REV. B. R. HALL.
THE TEACHER TAUGHT, by EMERSON DAVIS.
THE TEACHER, by ABBOTT.
LECTURES ON EDUCATION, by HORACE MANN.
SLATE AND BLACKBOARD EXERCISES, by DR. ALCOTT.
NORTHEND'S DICTATION EXERCISES.
UNIVERSAL EDUCATION, by IRA MAYHEW.
THE TEACHER'S INSTITUTE, by W. B. FOWLE.
EXERCISES FOR THE SENSES. (Chas. Knight: London.)
LESSONS ON OBJECTS, by C. MAYO. (London.)
FIVE HUNDRED MISTAKES.
LIVE AND LEARN.
GOOD'S BOOK OF NATURE.
MITCHELL'S PLANETARY AND STELLAR WORLDS.
COLTON'S PHYSICAL GEOGRAPHY.
BROCKLESBY'S METEOROLOGY.
TRENCH ON THE STUDY OF WORDS.
TRENCH'S ENGLISH, PAST AND PRESENT.
CALVERT'S SOCIAL SCIENCE.
PHILOSOPHY IN SPORT MADE SCIENCE IN EARNEST.
WILSON'S TREATISE ON PUNCTUATION.
ROGET'S THESAURUS OF ENGLISH WORDS.
PETERSON'S FAMILIAR SCIENCE.
DAVIES' PRACTICAL MATHEMATICS.
A LIFT FOR THE LAZY.
HARRISON ON THE ENGLISH LANGUAGE.
PORTER'S PRINCIPLES OF CHEMISTRY.
WELCH'S ANALYSIS OF THE ENGLISH SENTENCE.

N. B.—These books are not expensive, and are obtainable through any publisher.

ORTHOGRAPHY AND READING.

NATIONAL SERIES
OF
READERS AND SPELLERS,
BY PARKER & WATSON.

The National Primer	$ 25
National First Reader	38
National Second Reader	63
National Third Reader	95
National Fourth Reader	1 50
National Fifth Reader	1 88
National Elementary Speller	25
National Pronouncing Speller	45

This unrivaled series has acquired for itself during a very few years of publication, a reputation and circulation never before attained by a series of school readers in the same space of time. No contemporary books can be at all compared with them. The average annual *increase* in circulation exceeds 100,000 volumes. We challenge rival publishers to show such a record.

The salient features of these works which have combined to render them so popular may be briefly recapitulated as follows ;

1. THE WORD METHOD SYSTEM.—This famous progressive method for young children originated and was copyrighted with these books. It constitutes a process by which the beginner with *words* of one letter is gradually introduced to additional lists formed by prefixing or affixing single letters, and is thus led almost insensibly to the mastery of the more difficult constructions. This is justly regarded as one of the most striking modern improvements in methods of teaching.

2. TREATMENT OF PRONUNCIATION.—The wants of the youngest scholars in this department are not overlooked. It may be said that from the first lesson the student by this method need never be at a loss for a prompt and accurate rendering of every word encountered.

3. ARTICULATION AND ORTHOEPY are recognized as of primary importance.

(Over.)

ORTHOGRAPHY AND READING—Continued.

4. **PUNCTUATION** is inculcated by a series of interesting *reading lessons*, the simple perusal of which suffices to fix its principles indelibly upon the mind.

5. **ELOCUTION.** Each of the higher Readers (3d, 4th and 5th) contains elaborate, scholarly, and thoroughly practical treatises on elocution. This feature alone has secured for the series many of its warmest friends.

6. **THE SELECTIONS** are the crowning glory of the series. Without exception it may be said that no volumes of the same size and character contain a collection so diversified, judicious, and artistic as this. It embraces the choicest gems of English literature, so arranged as to afford the reader ample exercise in every department of style. So acceptable has the taste of the authors in this department proved, not only to the educational public but to the reading community at large, that thousands of copies of the Fourth and Fifth Readers have found their way into public and private libraries throughout the country, where they are in constant use as manuals of literature, for reference as well as perusal.

7. **ARRANGEMENT.** The exercises are so arranged as to present constantly alternating practice in the different styles of composition, while observing a definite plan of progression or gradation throughout the whole. In the higher books the articles are placed in formal sections and classified topically, thus concentrating the interest and inculcating a principle of association likely to prove valuable in subsequent general reading.

8. **NOTES AND BIOGRAPHICAL SKETCHES.** These are full and adequate to every want. The biographical sketches present in pleasing style the history of every author laid under contribution.

9. **ILLUSTRATIONS.** These are plentiful, almost profuse, and of the highest character of art. They are found in every volume of the series as far as and including the Third Reader.

10. **THE GRADATION** is perfect. Each volume overlaps its companion preceding or following in the series, so that the scholar, in passing from one to another, is barely conscious, save by the presence of the new book, of the transition.

11. **THE PRICE** is reasonable. The books were not *trimmed* to the minimum of size in order that the publishers might be able to denominate them "the cheapest in the market," but were made *large enough* to cover and suffice for the grade indicated by the respective numbers. Thus the child is not compelled to go over his First Reader twice, or be driven into the Second before he is prepared for it. The competent teachers who compiled the series made each volume just what it should be, leaving it for their brethren who should use the books to decide what constitutes true *cheapness*. A glance over the books will satisfy any one that the same amount of matter is nowhere furnished at a price more reasonable. Besides which another consideration enters into the question of relative economy, namely, the

12. **BINDING.** By the use of a material and process known only to themselves, in common with all the publications of this house, the National Readers are warranted to out-last any with which they may be compared—the ratio of relative durability being in their favor as two to one.

Parker & Watson's National Series of Readers.

TESTIMONIALS.

From HON. T A. PARKER, *State Sup't of Public Instruction, Missouri.*

By authority of law it becomes my duty to recommend a list of Text-books for use in the Public Schools of Missouri. I deem it necessary to approve a list of books which will secure to the youth of the State a *uniform, cheap, and practical* course of study, and after careful examination have selected the following: THE NATIONAL READERS AND SPELLERS, *Monteith & McNally's Geographies, Peck's Ganot's Natural Philosophy, Jarvis' Physiology and Health,* &c., &c.

From SAM'L P. BATES, LL.D., *Asst. Supt. Public Schools of Pennsylvania.*

I find that your series of Parker & Watson's National Readers are going into use in all our leading Normal Schools. They are unquestionably ahead of any thing yet published.

From A. J. HAILE, *Prin. Hebrew Educational Institute, Memphis, Tennessee.*

I take great pleasure in bearing testimony to the superior merits of Parker & Watson's Series of "National Readers."

From PROF. F. S. JEWELL, *of the New York State Normal School.*

It gives me pleasure to find in the National Series of School-Readers ample room for commendation From a brief examination, I am led to believe that we have none equal to them. I hope they will prove as popular as they are excellent.

From MOSES T. BROWN, *Superintendent Public Schools, Toledo, Ohio.*

The different Series of other authors were critically examined by our Board of Education and myself, and the decision was unanimous in favor of the National Series. Our teachers are delighted with the books, and none more so than our primary teachers. *I consider the Series better adapted to our graded school system than any other now before the public.*

From WM. B. AMES, *Superintendent of Schools, Morris, Connecticut.*

They are well adapted to all degrees of scholarship—one lesson prepares the mind of the pupil for the next in consecutive order, from book to book—till the highest order of English composition is attained in the Fifth Reader.

From JOHN S. HART, *Prin. N. J. State Normal School.*

I approve of Parker & Watson's Readers highly. The selections are judicious, the arrangement good, and the books well made mechanically. We have adopted the 3d, 4th, and 5th of the Series in this school.

From R. P. DECKARD, *President Ewing College, La Grange, Texas.*

I think the National Series of Readers the best I have seen.

Extracts from Report made to the California State Teachers' Association.

The Committee, in presenting to this Convention the Series of Readers by Parker & Watson, would state that, regarded as a whole, we would give our unqualified support to them in preference to all others.

From B. J. YOUNG, *Superintendent Schools, Shelbyville, Illinois.*

The National Readers have been selected for use in the public schools of this city, and are giving very excellent satisfaction. During ten years' experience in teaching, I have found no books so well adapted to secure rapid and thorough progress.

From the WILMINGTON (N. C.) DAILY HERALD.

The National Series has attained probably a higher reputation than any other complete series of School-Books in existence.

☞ For further testimony of a similar character, see special circular, or current numbers of the Educational Bulletin.

The National Readers and Spellers.

THEIR RECORD.

These books have been adopted by the School Boards, or official authority, of the following important States, cities, and towns—in most cases for exclusive use.

The State of Minnesota.

The State of Missouri.

New York.
New York City.
Brooklyn.
Buffalo.
Albany.
Rochester.
Troy.
Syracuse.
Elmira.
&c., &c.

Pennsylvania.
Reading.
Lancaster.
Erie.
Scranton.
Carlisle.
Carbondale.
Meadville.
Schuylkill Haven.
Williamsport.
Norristown.
Bellefonte.
Altoona.
&c., &c.

New Jersey.
Newark.
Jersey City.
Paterson.
Trenton.
Camden.
Elizabeth.
New Brunswick.
Phillipsburg.
Orange.
&c., &c.

Delaware.
Wilmington.

D. C.
Washington.

Illinois.
Chicago.
Peoria.
Alton.
Springfield.
Aurora.
Galesburg.
Rockford.
Rock Island.
&c., &c.

Wisconsin.
Milwaukee.
Fond du Lac.
Oshkosh.
Janesville.
Racine.
Watertown.
Sheboygan.
La Crosse.
Waukesha.
Kenosha.
&c., &c.

Michigan.
Grand Rapids.
Kalamazoo.
Adrian.
Jackson.
Monroe.
Lansing.
&c., &c.

Ohio.
Toledo.
Sandusky.
Conneaut.
Chardon.
Hudson.
Canton.
Salem.
&c., &c.

Indiana.
New Albany.
Fort Wayne.
Lafayette.
Madison.
Logansport.
&c., &c.

Iowa.
Davenport.
Burlington.
Muscatine.
Mount Pleasant.
&c.

California.
Sacramento.
Marysville.
&c.

Oregon.
Portland.
Salem.
&c.

*** Virginia.**
Richmond.
Norfolk.
Petersburg.
Lynchburg.
&c.

*** Carolina.**
Wilmington.
Charleston.

*** Georgia.**
Savannah.

*** Louisiana.**
New Orleans.

*** Tennessee.**
Memphis.

* With the organization and progress of common-school systems at the South, this list will, of course, be greatly increased. These points are, at present, almost the only ones enjoying the advantages of public schools. The National Readers are used in a large number of the best private schools and academies throughout the South.

The *Educational Bulletin* records periodically all new points gained.

SCHOOL-ROOM CARDS,

To Accompany the National Readers.

Eureka Alphabet Tablet *1 50

Presents the alphabet upon the Word Method System, by which the child will learn the alphabet in nine days, and make no small progress in reading and spelling in the same time.

National School Tablets, 10 Nos. *7 50

Embrace reading and conversational exercises, object and moral lessons, form, color, &c. A complete set of these large and elegantly illustrated Cards will embellish the school-room more than any other article of furniture.

READING.

Fowle's Bible Reader $1 00

The narrative portions of the Bible, chronologically and topically arranged, judiciously combined with selections from the Psalms, Proverbs, and other portions which inculcate important moral lessons or the great truths of Christianity. The embarrassment and difficulty of reading the Bible itself, by course, as a class exercise, are obviated, and its use made feasible, by this means.

North Carolina First Reader 50

North Carolina Second Reader 75

North Carolina Third Reader 1 00

Prepared expressly for the schools of this State, by C. H. Wiley, Superintendent of Common Schools, and F. M. Hubbard, Professor of Literature in the State University.

Parker's Rhetorical Reader 1 00

Designed to familiarize Readers with the pauses and other marks in general use, and lead them to the practice of modulation and inflection of the voice.

Introductory Lessons in Reading and Elocution 75

Of similar character to the foregoing, for less advanced classes.

High School Literature 1 50

Admirable selections from a long list of the world's best writers, for exercise in reading, oratory, and composition. Speeches, dialogues, and model letters represent the latter department.

ORTHOGRAPHY.

SMITH'S SERIES

Supplies a speller for every class in graded schools, and comprises the most complete and excellent treatise on English Orthography and its companion branches extant.

1. Smith's Little Speller . . . . $ 20

First Round in the Ladder of Learning.

2. Smith's Juvenile Definer 45

Lessons composed of familiar words grouped with reference to similar signification or use, and correctly spelled, accented, and defined.

3. Smith's Grammar-School Speller 50

Familiar words, grouped with reference to the sameness of sound of syllables differently spelled. Also definitions, complete rules for spelling and formation of derivatives, and exercises in false orthography.

4. Smith's Speller and Definer's Manual . 90

A complete *School Dictionary* containing 14,000 words, with various other useful matter in the way of Rules and Exercises.

5. Smith's Hand-Book of Etymology . . . 1 25

The first and only Etymology to recognize the *Anglo-Saxon* our *mother tongue;* containing also full lists of derivatives from the Latin, Greek, Gaelic, Swedish, Norman, &c., &c.; being, in fact, a complete etymology of the language for schools.

Sherwood's Writing Speller 15

Sherwood's Speller and Definer 15

Sherwood's Speller and Pronouncer . . . 15

The Writing Speller consists of properly ruled and numbered blanks to receive the words dictated by the teacher, with space for remarks and corrections. The other volumes may be used for the dictation or ordinary class exercises.

Price's English Speller *15

A complete spelling-book for all grades, containing more matter than "Webster," manufactured in superior style, and sold at a lower price—consequently the cheapest speller extant.

Northend's Dictation Exercises 63

Embracing valuable information on a thousand topics, communicated in such a manner as at once to relieve the exercise of spelling of its usual tedium, and combine it with instruction of a general character calculated to profit and amuse.

Wright's Analytical Orthography 25

This standard work is popular, because it teaches the elementary sounds in a plain and philosophical manner, and presents orthography and orthoepy in an easy, uniform system of analysis or parsing.

Fowle's False Orthography 45

Exercises for correction.

Page's Normal Chart *3 75

The elementary sounds of the language for the school-room walls.

ENGLISH GRAMMAR.

CLARK'S DIAGRAM SYSTEM.

Clark's First Lessons in Grammar . . . 50
Clark's English Grammar 1 00
Clark's Key to English Grammar 60
Clark's Analysis of the English Language . 60
Clark's Grammatical Chart 4 00

The theory and practice of teaching grammar in American schools is meeting with a thorough revolution from the use of this system. While the old methods offer proficiency to the pupil only after much weary plodding and dull memorizing, this affords from the inception the advantage of *practical Object Teaching*, addressing the eye by means of illustrative figures; furnishes association to the memory, its most powerful aid, and diverts the pupil by taxing his ingenuity. Teachers who are using Clark's Grammar uniformly testify that they and their pupils find it the most interesting study of the school course.

Like all great and radical improvements, the system naturally met at first with much unreasonable opposition. It has not only outlived the greater part of this opposition, but finds many of its warmest admirers among those who could not at first tolerate so radical an innovation. All it wants is an impartial trial, to convince the most skeptical of its merit. No one who has fairly and intelligently tested it in the school-room has ever been known to go back to the old method. A great success is already established, and it is easy to prophecy that the day is not far distant when it will be the *only system of teaching English Grammar.* As the SYSTEM is copyrighted, no other text-books can appropriate this obvious and great improvement.

Welch's Analysis of the English Sentence . 1 10

Remarkable for its new and simple classification, its method of treating connectives, its explanations of the idioms and constructive laws of the language, &c.

ETYMOLOGY.

Smith's Complete Etymology, ... 1 25

Containing the Anglo-Saxon, French, Dutch, German, Welsh, Danish, Gothic, Swedish, Gaelic, Italian, Latin, and Greek Roots, and the English words derived therefrom accurately spelled, accented, and defined.

The Topical Lexicon, ... 1 50

This work is a School Dictionary, an Etymology, a compilation of synonyms, and a manual of general information. It differs from the ordinary lexicon in being arranged by topics instead of the letters of the alphabet, thus realizing the apparent paradox of a "Readable Dictionary." An unusually valuable school-book.

Clark's Diagram English Grammar.

TESTIMONIALS.

From J. A. T. Durnin, *Principal Dubuque R. C. Academy, Iowa.*

In my opinion, it is well calculated by its system of analysis to develop those rational faculties which in the old systems were rather left to develop themselves, while the memory was overtaxed, and the pupils discouraged.

From B. A. Cox, *School Commissioner, Warren County, Illinois.*

I have examined 150 teachers in the last year, and those having studied or taught Clark's System have universally stood fifty per cent. better examinations than those having studied other authors.

From M. H. B. Burket, *Principal Masonic Institute, Georgetown, Tennessee.*

I traveled two years amusing myself in instructing (exclusively) Grammar classes with Clark's system. The first class I instructed fifty days, but found that this was more time than was required to impart a theoretical knowledge of the science. During the two years thereafter I instructed classes only *thirty* days each. Invariably I proposed that unless I prepared my classes for a more thorough, minute, and accurate knowledge of English Grammar than that obtained from the ordinary books and in the ordinary way in from one to two years, I would make no charge. I never failed in a solitary case to far exceed the hopes of my classes, and made money and character rapidly as an instructor.

From A. B. Douglass, *School Commissioner, Delaware County, New York.*

I have never known a class pursue the study of it under a *live* teacher, that has not succeeded; I have never known it to have an opponent in an educated teacher who had *thoroughly* investigated it; I have never known an *ignorant* teacher to examine it; I have never known a teacher who has used it, to try any other.

From J. A. Dodge, *Teacher and Lecturer on English Grammar, Kentucky.*

We are tempted to assert that it foretells the dawn of a brighter age to our mother-tongue. Both pupil and teacher can fare sumptuously upon its contents, however highly they may have prized the manuals into which they may have been initiated, and by which their expressions have been moulded.

From W. T. Chapman, *Superintendent Public Schools, Wellington, Ohio.*

I regard Clark's System of Grammar the best published. For teaching the analysis of the English Language, it surpasses any I ever used.

From F. S. Lyon, *Principal South Norwalk Union School, Connecticut.*

During ten years' experience in teaching, I have used six different authors on the subject of English Grammar. I am fully convinced that Clark's Grammar is better calculated to make thorough grammarians than any other that I have seen.

From Catalogue of Rohrer's Commercial College, *St. Louis, Missouri.*

We do not hesitate to assert, without fear of successful contradiction, that a better knowledge of the English language can be obtained by this system in six weeks than by the old methods in as many months.

From A. Pickett, *President of the State Teachers' Association, Wisconsin.*

A thorough experiment in the use of many approved authors upon the subject of English Grammar has convinced me of the superiority of Clark. When the pupil has completed the course, he is left upon a foundation of *principle*, and not upon the *dictum* of the author.

From Geo. F. McFarland, *Prin. McAllisterville Academy, Juniata Co., Penn.*

At the first examination of public-school teachers by the county superintendent, when one of our student teachers commenced analyzing a sentence according to Clark, the superintendent listened in mute astonishment until he had finished, then asked what that meant, and finally, with a very knowing look, said such work wouldn't do here, and asked the applicant to parse the sentence right, and gave the lowest certificates to all who barely mentioned Clark. Afterwards, I presented him with a copy, and the next fall he permitted it to be partially used, while the third or last fall, he openly commended the system, and appointed three of my best teachers to explain it at the two Institutes and one County Convention held since September.

☞ For further testimony of equal force, see the Publishers' Special Circular, or current numbers of the Educational Bulletin.

GEOGRAPHY.

THE

NATIONAL GEOGRAPHICAL SYSTEM.

I.	Monteith's First Lessons in Geography,	$ 35
II.	Monteith's Introduction to the Manual, .	65
III.	Monteith's New Manual of Geography, .	1 00
IV.	Monteith's Physical & Intermediate Geog.	1 75
V.	McNally's System of Geography, . . .	1 88

The only complete course of geographical instruction. Its circulation is almost universal—its merits patent. A few of the elements of its popularity are found in the following points of excellence.

1. PRACTICAL OBJECT TEACHING. The infant scholar is first introduced to *a picture* whence he may derive notions of the shape of the earth, the phenomena of day and night, the distribution of land and water, and the great natural divisions, which mere words would fail entirely to convey to the untutored mind. Other pictures follow on the same plan, and the child's mind is called upon to grasp no idea without the aid of a pictorial illustration. Carried on to the higher books, this system culminates in No. 4, where such matters as climates, ocean currents, the winds, peculiarities of the earth's crust, clouds and rain, are pictorially explained and rendered apparent to the most obtuse. The illustrations used for this purpose belong to the highest grade of art.

2. CLEAR, BEAUTIFUL, AND CORRECT MAPS. In the lower numbers the maps avoid unnecessary detail, while respectively progressive, and affording the pupil new matter for acquisition each time he approaches in the constantly enlarging circle the point of coincidence with previous lessons in the more elementary books. In No. 4, the maps embrace many new and striking features. One of the most effective of these is the new plan for displaying on each map the relative sizes of countries not represented, thus obviating much confusion which has arisen from the necessity of presenting maps in the same atlas drawn on different scales. The maps of No. 5 have long been celebrated for their superior beauty and completeness. This is the only school-book in which the attempt to make a *complete* atlas *also clear and distinct*, has been successful. The map *coloring* throughout the series is also noticeable. Delicate and subdued tints take the place of the startling glare of inharmonious colors which too frequently in such treatises dazzle the eyes, distract the attention, and serve to overwhelm the names of towns and the natural features of the landscape.

GEOGRAPHY—Continued

3. THE VARIETY OF MAP EXERCISE. Starting each time from a different basis, the pupil in many instances approaches the same fact no less than *six times*, thus indelibly impressing it upon his memory. At the same time this system is not allowed to become wearisome—the extent of exercise on each subject being graduated by its relative importance or difficulty of acquisition.

4. THE CHARACTER AND ARRANGEMENT OF THE DESCRIPTIVE TEXT. The cream of the science has been carefully culled, unimportant matter rejected, elaboration avoided, and a brief and concise manner of presentation cultivated. The orderly consideration of topics has contributed greatly to simplicity. Due attention is paid to the facts in history and astronomy which are inseparably connected with, and important to the proper understanding of geography—and *such only* are admitted on any terms. In a word, the National System teaches geography as a science, pure, simple, and exhaustive.

5. ALWAYS UP TO THE TIMES. The authors of these books, editorially speaking, never sleep. No change occurs in the boundaries of countries, or of counties, no new discovery is made, or railroad built, that is not at once noted and recorded, and the next edition of each volume carries to every school-room the new order of things.

6. SUPERIOR GRADATION. This is the only series which furnishes an available volume for every possible class in graded schools. It is not contemplated that a pupil must necessarily go through every volume in succession to attain proficiency. On the contrary, *two* will suffice, but *three* are advised; and if the course will admit, the whole series should be pursued. At all events, the books are at hand for selection, and every teacher, of every grade, can find among them one *exactly suited* to his class. The best combination for those who wish to abridge the course consists of Nos. 1, 3, and 5, or where children are somewhat advanced in other studies when they commence geography, Nos. 2, 3, and 5. Where but *two* books are admissible, Nos. 2 and 4, or Nos. 3 and 5, are recommended.

7. FORM OF THE VOLUMES AND MECHANICAL EXECUTION. The maps and text are no longer unnaturally divorced in accordance with the time-honored practice of making text-books on this subject as inconvenient and expensive as possible. On the contrary, all map questions are to be found on the page opposite the map itself, and each book is complete in one volume. The mechanical execution is unrivalled. Paper and printing are everything that could be desired, and the binding is—A. S. Barnes and Company's.

Ripley's Map Drawing $1 25

This system adopts the circle as its basis, abandoning the processes by triangulation, the square, parallels, and meridians, &c., which have been proved not feasible or natural in the development of this science. Success seems to indicate that the circle "has it."

National Outline Maps

For the school-room walls. In preparation.

Monteith & McNally's National Geographies.

TESTIMONIALS.

From O. F. Russell, *Principal Normal Academy, Arkansas.*

Before the war I used Monteith and McNally's Geographies, and do not hesitate to pronounce them the best that ever came under my observation.

From Hamilton McAfee, *Superintendent Caldwell County, Missouri.*

Monteith and McNally's Geographies are superior to any in use; in point of mechanical execution they are certainly unrivaled.

From E. W. Peet, *Principal Walworth County Institute, Wisconsin.*

We have used Monteith's Geographies in the Institute for two years, where they have given the best satisfaction. I most heartily indorse and recommend them.

From Joseph Peabody, *Principal Moody School, Lowell, Massachusetts.*

I have examined Monteith's Geographies carefully, and feel confident in saying that they are *the best series of Geographies* that have come under my observation.

From Rev. B. St. James Fry, A.M., *President Worthington Female College, Ohio.*

We have used McNally and Monteith's Geographies for three years, and would not exchange them for any others in the market.

From R. M. Magee, *Superintendent Centre County, Pennsylvania.*

Monteith and McNally's Geographies have been examined carefully, and I am free to say I think they are superior in many respects to any other system.

From W. L. Alexander, *President Nacogdoches College, Texas.*

I regard as perfect, in every respect, "Monteith and McNally's Geographical Series."

From C. P. De Hass, *Principal North Hill Public School, Burlington, Iowa.*

I favored the adoption of Monteith and McNally's Series of Geographies, because I liked them; and now, after nearly a year's trial of them in the school-room, I like them better than ever.

From R. A. Adams, *Member of Board of Education, New York.*

I have found, by examination of the Book of Supply of our Board, that considerably the largest number of any series now used in our public schools is the National, by Monteith and McNally.

From Josiah T. Reade, *Principal Union School, Marshall, Michigan.*

This series was adopted after a careful examination of the best works in this branch of study, and a year's experience makes us better and better satisfied with our choice.

From Emory F. Strong, *Principal High School, Bridgeport, Connecticut.*

We are using, with very great satisfaction, in the school with which I am connected, Monteith and McNally's Geographies. Other schools in this city are using them with the same favorable opinion of their merits.

From A. R. McGill, *Superintendent Nicollet County, Minnesota.*

I am happy to express my hearty approval of the *Series throughout.*

From James N. Townsend, *Superintendent Public Schools, Hudson, New York.*

I have *carefully* examined your series of Monteith and McNally's Geographies. They are comprehensive, accurate, well graded, handsomely gotten up, *complete.* I am frank to confess that I consider it by far the best series ever published in this country. They are unrivaled. We have recently adopted them in the public schools of this city, to the infinite delight of the students, and to the entire satisfaction of the teachers.

☞ For further testimony of similar character, see the Publishers' special circular, or current numbers of the Educational Bulletin.

The National System of Geography,

By Monteith & McNally.

ITS RECORD.

These popular text-books have been adopted, by official authority, for the schools of the following States, cities, and associations—in most cases for exclusive and uniform use.

Minnesota.	By State Board of Education.	
Vermont.	Do.	do.
Missouri.	By State Superintendent of Common Schools.	
Iowa.	Do.	do.
Kansas.	Do.	do.
Virginia.	By State Teachers' Convention.	
Mississippi.	Do.	do.
Texas.	Do.	do.

☞ This li[illegible] includes nearly every State in which official recommendation is made.

New York City.	Louisville.
Brooklyn.	Newark.
New Orleans.	Milwaukee.
Buffalo.	Charleston.
Richmond.	Rochester.
Jersey City.	Mobile.
Hartford.	Syracuse.
Worcester.	Memphis.
Utica.	Savannah.
Wilmington.	Indianapolis.
Trenton.	Springfield.
Norfolk.	Wheeling.
Norwich.	Toledo.
Lockport.	Bridgeport.
Dubuque.	St. Paul.

And a multitude of less important points.

The Society of the Christian Brothers, representing 40,000 pupils.
The Franciscan Brothers, 8,000 pupils.
American Missionary Society, 50,000 pupils.

THE FREEDMEN,

By State Superintendents under the Freedmen's Bureau of

North Carolina.	*Georgia.*
Louisiana.	*Texas.*

For New triumphs of these truly *National* books, see current numbers of the Educational Bulletin.

MATHEMATICS.

DAVIES' NATIONAL COURSE.

ARITHMETIC.

1. Davies' Primary Arithmetic . . . . $ 25
2. Davies' Intellectual Arithmetic 40
3. Davies' Elements of Written Arithmetic 50
4. Davies' Practical Arithmetic 1 00
   Key to Practical Arithmetic *1 00
5. Davies' University Arithmetic 1 50
   Key to University Arithmetic *1 50

ALGEBRA.

1. Davies' New Elementary Algebra 1 25
   Key to Elementary Algebra *1 25
2. Davies' University Algebra 1 60
   Key to University Algebra *1 60
3. Davies' Bourdon's Algebra 2 25
   Key to Bourdon's Algebra *2 25

GEOMETRY.

1. Davies' Elementary Geometry and Trigonometry . 1 40
2. Davies' Legendre's Geometry 2 25
3. Davies' Analytical Geometry and Calculus 2 50
4. Davies' Descriptive Geometry 2 75

MENSURATION.

1. Davies' Practical Mathematics and Mensuration . . 1 40
2. Davies' Surveying and Navigation 2 50
3. Davies' Shades, Shadows, and Perspective 3 75

MATHEMATICAL SCIENCE.

Davies' Grammar of Arithmetic . . . . * 50
Davies' Outlines of Mathematical Science *1 00
Davies' Logic and Utility of Mathematics *1 50
Davies & Peck's Dictionary of Mathematics . *3 75

DAVIES' NATIONAL COURSE of MATHEMATICS.

ITS RECORD.

In claiming for this series the first place among American text-books, of whatever class, the Publishers appeal to the magnificent record which its volumes have earned during the *thirty-five years* of Dr. Charles Davies' mathematical labors. The unremitting exertions of a life-time have placed *the modern series* on the same proud eminence among competitors that each of its predecessors has successively enjoyed in a course of constantly improved editions, now rounded to their perfect fruition—for it seems indeed that this science is susceptible of no further demonstration.

During the period alluded to, many authors and editors in this department have started into public notice, and by borrowing ideas and processes original with Dr. Davies, have enjoyed a brief popularity, but are now almost unknown. Many of the series of to-day, built upon a similar basis, and described as "modern books," are destined to a similar fate; while the most far-seeing eye will find it difficult to fix the time, on the basis of any data afforded by their past history, when these books will cease to increase and prosper, and fix a still firmer hold on the affection of every educated American.

One cause of this unparalleled popularity is found in the fact that the enterprise of the author did not cease with the original completion of his books. Always a practical teacher, he has incorporated in his text-books from time to time the advantages of every improvement in methods of teaching, and every advance in science. During all the years in which he has been laboring, he constantly submitted his own theories and those of others to the practical test of the class-room—approving, rejecting, or modifying them as the experience thus obtained might suggest. In this way he has been able to produce an almost perfect series of class-books, in which every department of mathematics has received minute and exhaustive attention.

Nor has he yet retired from the field. Still in the prime of life, and enjoying a ripe experience which no other living mathematician or teacher can emulate, his pen is ever ready to carry on the good work, as the progress of science may demand. Witness his recent exposition of the "Metric System," which received the official endorsement of Congress, by its Committee on Uniform Weights and Measures.

DAVIES' SYSTEM IS THE ACKNOWLEDGED NATIONAL STANDARD FOR THE UNITED STATES, for the following reasons:—

1st. It is the basis of instruction in the great national schools at West Point and Annapolis.

2d. It has received the *quasi* endorsement of the National Congress.

3d. It is exclusively used in the public schools of the National Capital.

4th. The officials of the Government use it as authority in all cases involving mathematical questions.

5th. Our great soldiers and sailors commanding the national armies and navies were educated in this system. So have been a majority of eminent scientists in this country. All these refer to "Davies" as authority.

6th. A larger number of American citizens have received their education from this than from any other series.

7th. The series has a larger circulation throughout the whole country than any other, being *extensively used in every State in the Union.*

MATHEMATICS—Continued.

ARITHMETICAL EXAMPLES.

Reuck's Examples in Denominate Numbers $ 50

Reuck's Examples in Arithmetic 1 00

These volumes differ from the ordinary arithmetic in their peculiarly *practical* character. They are composed mainly of examples, and afford the most severe and thorough discipline for the mind. While a book which should contain a complete treatise of theory and practice would be too cumbersome for every-day use, the insufficiency of *practical* examples has been a source of complaint.

HIGHER MATHEMATICS.

Church's Elements of Calculus 2 50

Church's Analytical Geometry 2 50

Church's Descriptive Geometry, with Shades, Shadows, and Perspective 4 50

These volumes constitute the "West Point Course" in their several departments.

Courtenay's Elements of Calculus 3 25

A work especially popular at the South.

Hackley's Trigonometry 3 00

With applications to navigation and surveying, nautical and practical geometry and geodesy, and logarithmic, trigonometrical, and nautical tables.

THE METRIC SYSTEM.

The International System of Uniform Weights and Measures must hereafter be taught in all common-schools. Professor Charles Davies is the official exponent of the system, as indicated by the following resolutions, adopted by the Committee of the House of Representatives, on a "Uniform System of Coinage, Weights, and Measures," February 2, 1867:—

Resolved, That this committee has observed with gratification the efforts made by the editors and publishers of several mathematical works, designed for the use of common-schools and other institutions of learning, to introduce the Metric System of Weights and Measures, as authorized by Congress, into the system of instruction of the youth of the United States, in its various departments; and, in order to extend further the knowledge of its advantages, alike in public education and in general use by the people,

Be it further resolved, That Professor Charles Davies, LL.D., of the State of New York, be requested to confer with superintendents of public instruction, and teachers of schools, and others interested in a reform of the present incongruous system, and, by lectures and addresses, to promote its general introduction and use.

The official version of the Metric System, as prepared by Dr. Davies, may be found in the Written, Practical, and University Arithmetics of the Mathematical Series, and is also published separately, price postpaid, *five cents.*

Davies' National Course of Mathematics.

TESTIMONIALS.

From L. Van Bokkelen, *State Superintendent Public Instruction, Maryland.*

The series of Arithmetics edited by Prof. Davies, and published by your firm, have been used for many years in the schools of several counties, and the city of Baltimore, and have been approved by teachers and commissioners.

Under the law of 1865, establishing a uniform system of Free Public Schools, these Arithmetics were unanimously adopted by the State Board of Education, after a careful examination, and are now used in all the Public Schools of Maryland.

These facts evidence the high opinion entertained by the School Authorities of the value of the series theoretically and practically.

From Horace Webster, *President of the College of New York.*

The undersigned has examined, with care and thought, several volumes of Davies' Mathematics, and is of the opinion that, as a whole, it is the most complete and best course for Academic and Collegiate instruction with which he is acquainted.

From David N. Camp, *State Superintendent of Common Schools, Connecticut.*

I have examined Davies' Series of Arithmetics with some care. The language is clear and precise; each principle is thoroughly analyzed, and the whole so arranged as to facilitate the work of instruction. Having observed the satisfaction and success with which the different books have been used by eminent teachers, it gives me pleasure to commend them to others.

From J. O. Wilson, *Chairman Committee on Text-Books, Washington, D. C.*

I consider Davies' Arithmetics decidedly superior to any other series, and in this opinion I am sustained, I believe, by the entire Board of Education and Corps of Teachers in this city, where they have been used for several years past.

From John L. Campbell, *Professor of Mathematics, Wabash College, Indiana.*

A proper combination of abstract reasoning and practical illustration is the chief excellence in Prof. Davies' Mathematical works. I prefer his Arithmetics, Algebras, Geometry, and Trigonometry to all others now in use, and cordially recommend them to all who desire the advancement of sound learning.

From Major J. H. Whittlesey, *Government Inspector of Military Schools.*

Be assured I regard the works of Professor Davies, with which I am acquainted, as by far the best text-books in print on the subjects which they treat. I shall certainly encourage their adoption wherever a word from me may be of any avail.

From T. McC. Ballantine, *Professor Mathematics, Cumberland College, Kentucky.*

I have long taught Prof. Davies' Course of Mathematics, and I continue to like their working.

From John McLean Bell, B. A., *Principal of Lower Canada College.*

I have used Davies' Arithmetical and Mathematical Series as text-books in the schools under my charge for the last six years. These I have found of great efficacy in exciting, invigorating, and concentrating the intellectual faculties of the young.

Each treatise serves as an introduction to the next higher, by the similarity of its reasonings and methods; and the student is carried forward, by easy and gradual steps, over the whole field of mathematical inquiry, and that, too, in a *shorter* time than is usually occupied in mastering a single department. I sincerely and heartily recommend them to the attention of my fellow-teachers in Canada.

From D. W. Steele, *Prin. Philekoian Academy, Cold Springs, Texas.*

I have used Davies' Arithmetics till I know them nearly by heart. A better series of school-books never were published. I have recommended them until they are now used in all this region of country.

A large mass of similar "Opinions" may be obtained by addressing the publishers for special circular for Davies' Mathematics. New recommendations are published in current numbers of the *Educational Bulletin.*

HISTORY.

Monteith's Youth's History, ...$ 75

A History of the United States for beginners. It is arranged upon the catechetical plan, with illustrative maps and engravings, review questions, dates in parentheses (that their study may be optional with the younger class of learners), and interesting Biographical Sketches of all persons who have been prominently identified with the history of our country.

Willard's United States, School edition, . . . 1 25
Do. do. University edition, . 2 25

The plan of this standard work is chronologically exhibited in front of the title-page; the Maps and Sketches are found useful assistants to the memory, and dates, usually so difficult to remember, are so systematically arranged as in a great degree to obviate the difficulty. Candor, impartiality, and accuracy, are the distinguishing features of the narrative portion.

Willard's Universal History, ... 2 25

The most valuable features of the "United States" are reproduced in this. The peculiarities of the work are its great conciseness and the prominence given to the chronological order of events. The margin marks each successive era with great distinctness, so that the pupil retains not only the event but its time, and thus fixes the order of history firmly and usefully in his mind. Mrs. Willard's books are constantly revised, and at all times written up to embrace important historical events of recent date.

Berard's History of England, ... 1 50

By an authoress well known for the success of her History of the United States. The social life of the English people is felicitously interwoven, as in fact, with the civil and military transactions of the realm.

Ricord's History of Rome, ... 1 25

Possesses the charm of an attractive romance. The Fables with which this history abounds are introduced in such a way as not to deceive the inexperienced, while adding materially to the value of the work as a reliable index to the character and institutions, as well as the history of the Roman people.

Hanna's Bible History, ... 1 25

The only compendium of Bible narrative which affords a connected and chronological view of the important events there recorded, divested of all superfluous detail.

Alison's History of Europe 2 50

An abridgment for Schools, by Gould, of this great standard work, covering the eventful period from A. D. 1789 to 1815, being mainly a history of the career of Napoleon.

Marsh's Ecclesiastical History, ... 1 88
Questions to ditto, ... 75

Affording the History of the Church in all ages, with accounts of the pagan world during Biblical periods, and the character, rise, and progress of all Religions, as well as the various sects of the worshipers of Christ. The work is entirely non-sectarian, though strictly catholic.

PENMANSHIP.

Beers' System of Progressive Penmanship.
Per dozen $2 50

This "round hand" system of penmanship in twelve numbers commends itself by its simplicity and thoroughness. The first four numbers are primary books. Nos. 5 to 7, advanced books for boys. Nos. 8 to 10 advanced books for girls. Nos. 11 and 12, ornamental penmanship. These books are printed from steel plates (engraved by McLees), and are unexcelled in mechanical execution. Large quantities are annually sold.

Beers' Slated Copy Slips, per set *50

All beginners should practice, for a few weeks, slate exercises, familiarizing them with the form of the letters, the motions of the hand and arm, &c., &c. These copy slips, 32 in number, supply all the copies found in a complete series of writing-books, at a trifling cost.

Fulton & Eastman's Copy Books, per dozen 1 50

A series for the economical,—complete in three numbers. (1) Elementary Exercises: (2) Gentlemen's Hand: (3) Ladies' Hand.

Fulton & Eastman's Chirographic Charts,
2 Nos., per set *5 00

To embellish the school-room walls, and furnish class exercise in the elements of Penmanship.

DRAWING.

Clark's Elements of Drawing 1 00

Containing full instructions, with appropriate designs and copies for a complete course in this graceful art, from the first rudiments of outline to the finished sketches of landscape and scenery.

Fowle's Linear and Perspective Drawing 60

For the cultivation of the eye and hand, with copious illustrations and directions which will enable the unskilled teacher to learn the art himself while instructing his pupils.

Monk's Drawing Books—Six Numbers, each, .* 40

A series of progressive Drawing Books, presenting copy and blank on opposite pages. The copies are fac-similes of the best imported lithographs, the originals of which cost from 50 cents to $1.50 *each* in the print-stores. Each book contains *eleven* large patterns. No. 1.—Elementary studies; No. 2.—Studies of Foliage; No. 3.—Landscapes; No. 4.—Animals, I.; No. 5.—Animals, II.; No. 6.—Marine Views, &c.

Ripley's Map Drawing 1 25

One of the most efficient aids to the acquirement of a knowledge of geography is the practice of map drawing. It is useful for the same reason that the best exercise in orthography is the *writing* of difficult words. Sight comes to the aid of hearing, and a double impression is produced upon the memory. Knowledge becomes less mechanical and more intuitive. The student who has sketched the outlines of a country, and dotted the important places, is little likely to forget either. The impression produced may be compared to that of a traveler who has been over the ground—while more comprehensive and accurate in detail.

ELOCUTION.

Northend's Little Orator *60

Contains simple and attractive pieces in prose and poetry, adapted to the capacity of children under twelve years of age.

Northend's National Orator *1 10

About one hundred and seventy choice pieces happily arranged. The design of the author in making the selection has been to cultivate *versatility of expression.*

Northend's Entertaining Dialogues *1 10

Extracts eminently adapted to cultivate the dramatic faculties, as well as entertain an audience.

Zachos' Analytic Elocution 1 25

All departments of elocution—such as the analysis of the voice and the sentence, phonology, rhythm, expression, gesture, &c.—are here arranged for instruction in classes, illustrated by copious examples.

Sherwood's Self Culture 1 25

Self culture in reading, speaking, and conversation—a very valuable treatise to those who would perfect themselves in these accomplishments.

BOOK-KEEPING.

Smith & Martin's Book-keeping 1 10
Blanks to ditto *60

This work is by a practical teacher and a practical book-keeper. It is of a thoroughly popular class, and will be welcomed by every one who loves to see theory and practice combined in an easy, concise, and methodical form.

The Single Entry portion is well adapted to supply a want felt in nearly all other treatises, which seem to be prepared mainly for the use of wholesale merchants, leaving retailers, mechanics, farmers, &c., who transact the greater portion of the business of the country, without a guide. The work is also commended on this account for general use in Young Ladies' seminaries, where a thorough grounding in the simpler form of accounts will be invaluable to the future housekeepers of the nation.

The treatise on Double Entry Book-keeping combines all the advantages of the most recent methods, with the utmost simplicity of application, thus affording the pupil all the advantages of actual experience in the counting-house, and giving a clear comprehension of the entire subject through a judicious course of mercantile transactions.

The shape of the book is such that the transactions can be presented as in actual practice; and the simplified form of Blanks, three in number, adds greatly to the case experienced in acquiring the science.

NATURAL SCIENCE.

FAMILIAR SCIENCE

Norton & Porter's First Book of Science, . $1 50

By eminent Professors of Yale College. Contains the principles of Natural Philosophy, Astronomy, Chemistry, Physiology, and Geology. Arranged on the Catechetical plan for primary classes and beginners.

Chambers' Treasury of Knowledge, . . . 1 10

Progressive lessons upon—*first*, common things which lie most immediately around us, and first attract the attention of the young mind; *second*, common objects from the Mineral, Animal, and Vegetable kingdoms, manufactured articles, and miscellaneous substances; *third*, a systematic view of Nature under the various sciences. May be used as a Reader or Text-Book.

NATURAL PHILOSOPHY.

Norton's First Book in Natural Philosophy, 90

By Prof. Norton, of Yale College. Designed for beginners; profusely illustrated, and arranged on the Catechetical plan.

Peck's Ganot's Course of Nat. Philosophy, 1 75

The standard text-book of France, Americanized and popularized by Prof. Peck, of Columbia College. The most magnificent system of illustration ever adopted in an American school-book is here found. For intermediate classes.

Peck's Elements of Mechanics, ... 2 25

A suitable introduction to Bartlett's higher treatises on Mechanical Philosophy, and adequate in itself for a complete academical course.

Bartlett's Synthetic Mechanics, ... 3 75

Bartlett's Analytical Mechanics, ... 5 50

Bartlett's Acoustics and Optics, ... 2 75

A system of Collegiate Philosophy, by Prof. Bartlett, of West Point Military Academy.

GEOLOGY.

Page's Elements of Geology, ... 1 10

A volume of Chambers' Educational Course. Practical, simple, and eminently calculated to make the study interesting.

Emmon's Manual of Geology, ... 1 25

The first Geologist of the country has here produced a work worthy of his reputation. The plan of presenting the subject is an obvious improvement on older methods. The department of Palæontology receives especial attention.

Peck's Ganot's Popular Physics.

TESTIMONIALS.

From PROF. ALONZO COLLIN, *Cornell College, Iowa.*

I am pleased with it. I have decided to introduce it as a text-book.

From H. F. JOHNSON, *President Madison College, Sharon, Miss.*

I am pleased with Peck's Ganot, and think it a magnificent book.

From PROF. EDWARD BROOKS, *Pennsylvania State Normal School*

So eminent are its merits, that it will be introduced as the text-book upon elementary physics in this institution.

From H. H. LOCKWOOD, *Professor Natural Philosophy U. S. Naval Academy.*

I am so pleased with it that I will probably add it to a course of lectures given to the midshipmen of this school on physics.

From GEO. S. MACKIE, *Professor Natural History University of Nashville, Tenn.*

I have decided on the introduction of Peck's Ganot's Philosophy, as I am satisfied that it is the best book for the purposes of my pupils that I have seen, combining simplicity of explanation with elegance of illustration.

From W. S. MCRAE, *Superintendent Vevay Public Schools, Indiana.*

Having carefully examined a number of text-books on natural philosophy, I do not hesitate to express my decided opinion in favor of Peck's Ganot. The matter, style, and illustration eminently adapt the work to the popular wants.

From REV. SAMUEL MCKINNEY, D.D., *President Austin College, Huntsville, Texas.*

It gives me pleasure to commend it to teachers. I have taught some classes with it as our text, and must say, for simplicity of style and clearness of illustration, I have found nothing as yet published of equal value to the teacher and pupil.

From C. V. SPEAR, *Principal Maplewood Institute, Pittsfield, Mass.*

I am much pleased with its ample illustrations by plates, and its clearness and simplicity of statement. It covers the ground usually gone over by our higher classes, and contains many fresh illustrations from life or daily occurrences and new applications of scientific principles to such.

From J. A. BANFIELD, *Superintendent Marshall Public Schools, Michigan.*

I have used Peck's Ganot since 1863, and with increasing pleasure and satisfaction each term. I consider it superior to any other work on physics in its adaptation to our high schools and academies. Its illustrations are superb—better than three times their number of pages of fine print.

From A. SCHUYLER, *Professor of Mathematics in Baldwin University, Berea, Ohio.*

After a careful examination of Peck's Ganot's Natural Philosophy, and an actual test of its merits as a text-book, I can heartily recommend it as admirably adapted to meet the wants of the grade of students for which it intended. Its diagrams and illustrations are *unrivaled.* We use it in the Baldwin University.

From D. C. VAN NORMAN, *Principal Van Norman Institute, New York.*

The Natural Philosophy of M. Ganot, edited by Prof. Peck, is, in my opinion, the best work of its kind, for the use intended, ever published in this country. Whether regarded in relation to the natural order of the topics, the precision and clearness of its definitions, or the fullness and beauty of its illustrations, it is certainly, I think, an advance.

☞ For many similar testimonials, see current numbers of the Illustrated Educational Bulletin.

NATURAL SCIENCE—Continued.

CHEMISTRY.

Porter's First Book of Chemistry, ... $ 90

Porter's Principles of Chemistry, ... 1 88

The above are widely known as the productions of one of the most eminent scientific men of America. The extreme simplicity in the method of presenting the science, while exhaustively treated, has excited universal commendation. Apparatus adequate to the performance of every experiment mentioned, may be had of the publishers for a trifling sum. The effort to popularize the science is a great success. It is now within the reach of the poorest and least capable at once.

Darby's Text-Book of Chemistry, ... 1 60

Purely a Chemistry, divesting the subject of matters comparatively foreign to it (such as heat, light, electricity, etc.), but usually allowed to engross too much attention in ordinary school-books.

Gregory's Organic Chemistry, ... 2 50

Gregory's Inorganic Chemistry, ... 2 50

The science exhaustively treated. For colleges and medical students.

Steele's Fourteen Weeks' Course, ... 1 25

A successful effort to reduce the study to the limits of a *single term*, thereby making feasible its general introduction in institutions of every character The author's felicity of style and success in making the science pre-eminently *interesting* are peculiarly noticeable features

Chemical Apparatus, ... *12 00

Comprising articles adequate for the practical illustration of the experiments in *Porter's* or *Steele's Chemistry*.

BOTANY.

Thinker's First Lessons in Botany, ... 40

For children. The technical terms are largely dispensed with in favor of an easy and familiar style adapted to the smallest learner.

Wood's Object Lessons in Botany, ... 1 40

Wood's Intermediate Botany, ... 2 25

Wood's New Class-Book of Botany, . . . 3 50

The standard text-books of the United States in this department. In style they are simple, popular, and lively; in arrangement, easy and natural; in description, graphic and strictly exact. The Tables for Analysis are reduced to a perfect system. More are annually sold than of all others combined.

Darby's Southern Botany, ... 2 00

Embracing general Structural and Physiological Botany, with vegetable products, and descriptions of Southern plants, and a complete Flora of the Southern States.

NATURAL SCIENCE—Continued

PHYSIOLOGY.

Jarvis' Primary Physiology, ... $ 75

Jarvis' Physiology and Laws of Health, . 1 50

The only books extant which approach this subject with a proper view of the true object of teaching Physiology in schools, viz., that scholars may know how to take care of their own health. In bold contrast with the abstract *Anatomies*, which children learn as they would Greek or Latin (and forget as soon), to *discipline the mind*, are these text-books, using the *science* as a secondary consideration, and only so far as is necessary for the comprehension of the *laws of health.*

Hamilton's Vegetable & Animal Physiology, 1 10

The two branches of the science combined in one volume lead the student to a proper comprehension of the Analogies of Nature.

ASTRONOMY.

Willard's School Astronomy, ... 90

By means of clear and attractive illustrations, addressing the eye in many cases by analogies, careful definitions of all necessary technical terms, a careful avoidance of verbiage and unimportant matter, particular attention to analysis, and a general adoption of the simplest methods, Mrs. Willard has made the best and most attractive *elementary* Astronomy extant.

McIntyre's Astronomy and the Globes, . . 1 25

A complete treatise for intermediate classes. Highly approved.

Bartlett's Spherical Astronomy, ... 4 50

The West Point course, for advanced classes, with applications to the current wants of Navigation, Geography, and Chronology.

NATURAL HISTORY.

Carl's Child's Book of Natural History, . . 0 50

Illustrating the Animal, Vegetable, and Mineral Kingdoms, with application to the Arts. For beginners. Beautifully and copiously illustrated.

ZOOLOGY.

Chambers' Elements of Zoology, ... 1 50

A complete and comprehensive system of Zoology, adapted for academic instruction, presenting a systematic view of the Animal Kingdom as a portion of external Nature.

☞ It will be observed, that, in the various departments of Natural Science, the NATIONAL SERIES is extremely rich. The mineral, animal, and vegetable kingdoms, matter, and the laws that govern it in all its forms, are here placed before the student by those who have made its study a specialty and a life work. The works of Professors PECK, of Columbia College, NORTON AND PORTER, of Yale, BARTLETT, of West Point Military Academy, EMMENS, of Williams, and State Geologist of New York and North Carolina, WOOD, the botanist, and JARVIS, the eminent physician, are esteemed indubitable authority in all that concerns their several specialties

Jarvis' Physiology and Laws of Health.

TESTIMONIALS.

From SAMUEL B. MCLANE, *Superintendent Public Schools, Keokuk, Iowa.*

I am glad to see a really good text-book on this much neglected branch. This is clear, concise, accurate, and eminently adapted to the *class-room.*

From WILLIAM F. WYERS, *Principal of Academy, West Chester, Pennsylvania.*

A thorough examination has satisfied me of its superior claims as a text-book to the attention of teacher and taught. I shall introduce it at once.

From H. R. SANFORD, *Principal of East Genesee Conference Seminary, N. Y.*

"Jarvis' Physiology" is received, and fully met our expectations. We immediately adopted it.

From ISAAC T. GOODNOW, *State Superintendent of Kansas—published in connection with the "School Law."*

"Jarvis' Physiology," a common-sense, practical work, with just enough of anatomy to understand the physiological portions. The last six pages, on Man's Responsibility for his own health, are worth the price of the book.

From D. W. STEVENS, *Superintendent Public Schools, Fall River, Mass.*

I have examined Jarvis' "Physiology and Laws of Health," which you had the kindness to send to me a short time ago. In my judgment it is far the best work of the kind within my knowledge. It has been adopted as a text-book in our public schools.

From HENRY G. DENNY, *Chairman Book Committee, Boston, Mass.*

The very excellent "Physiology" of Dr. Jarvis I had introduced into our High School, where the study had been temporarily dropped, believing it to be by far the best work of the kind that had come under my observation; indeed, the reintroduction of the study was delayed for some months, because Dr. Jarvis' book could not be had, and we were unwilling to take any other.

From PROF. A. P. PEABODY, D.D., LL.D., *Harvard University.*

* * I have been in the habit of examining school-books with great care, and I hesitate not to say that, of all the text-books on Physiology which have been given to the public, Dr. Jarvis' deserves the first place on the score of accuracy, thoroughness, method, simplicity of statement, and constant reference to topics of practical interest and utility.

From JAMES N. TOWNSEND, *Superintendent Public Schools, Hudson, N. Y.*

Every human being is appointed to take charge of his own body; and of all books written upon this subject, I know of none which will so well prepare one to do this as "Jarvis' Physiology"—that is, in so small a compass of matter. It considers the pure, simple *laws of health* paramount to science; and though the work is thoroughly scientific, it is divested of all cumbrous technicalities, and presents the subject of physical life in a manner and style really charming. It is unquestionably the best textbook on physiology I have ever seen. It is giving great satisfaction in the schools of this city, where it has been adopted as the standard.

From L. J. SANFORD, M.D., *Prof. Anatomy and Physiology in Yale College.*

Books on human physiology, designed for the use of schools, are more generally a failure perhaps than are school-books on most other subjects.

The great want in this department is met, we think, in the well-written treatise of Dr. Jarvis, entitled "Physiology and Laws of Health." * * The work is not too detailed nor too expansive in any department, and is clear and concise in all. It is not burdened with an excess of anatomical description, nor rendered discursive by many zoological references. Anatomical statements are made to the extent of qualifying the student to attend, understandingly, to an exposition of those functional processes which, collectively, make up health; thus the laws of health are enunciated, and many suggestions are given which, if heeded, will tend to its preservation.

☞ For further testimony of similar character, see current numbers of the **Illustrated** Educational Bulletin.

MODERN LANGUAGE.

French and English Primer, ... $ 10
German and English Primer, ... 10
Spanish and English Primer, ... 10

The names of common objects properly illustrated and arranged in easy lessons.

Ledru's French Fables, ... 75
Ledru's French Grammar, ... 1 00
Ledru's French Reader, ... 1 00

The author's long experience has enabled him to present the most thoroughly practical text-books extant, in this branch. The system of pronunciation (by phonetic illustration) is original with this author, and will commend itself to all American teachers, as it enables their pupils to secure an absolutely correct pronunciation without the assistance of a native master. This feature is peculiarly valuable also to "self-taught" students. The directions for ascertaining the gender of French nouns—also a great stumbling-block—are peculiar to this work, and will be found remarkably competent to the end proposed. The criticism of teachers and the test of the school-room is invited to this excellent series, with confidence.

Haskin's French and English First Book . 75

Presents the striking feature of a simultaneous presentation of the elementary principles of the vernacular with those of a foreign language. This is the method which the practical teacher naturally pursues in oral instruction, and possesses peculiar advantages in application to young pupils.

Pujol's Complete French Class-Book, . . . 2 25

Offers, in one volume, methodically arranged, a complete French course—usually embraced in series of from five to twelve books, including the bulky and expensive Lexicon. Here are Grammar, Conversation, and choice Literature—selected from the best French authors. Each branch is thoroughly handled; and the student, having diligently completed the course as prescribed, may consider himself, without further application, *au fait* in the most polite and elegant language of modern times.

Maurice-Poitevin's Grammaire Francaise, . 1 00

American schools are at last supplied with an American edition of this famous text-book. Many of our best institutions have for years been procuring it from abroad rather than forego the advantages it offers. The policy of putting students who have acquired some proficiency from the ordinary text-books, into a Grammar written in the vernacular, can not be too highly commended. It affords an opportunity for finish and review at once; while embodying abundant practice of its own rules.

Worman's Elementary German Grammar, . 1 12

A work of great merit. Well calculated to ground the student in the elements of this language, become so important by the extensive settlement of Germans in this country.

Willard's Historia de los Estados Unidos, . 2 00

The History of the United States, translated by Professors Tolon and De Tornos, will be found a valuable, instructive, and entertaining reading-book for Spanish classes.

Pujol's Complete French Class-Book.

TESTIMONIALS.

From PROF. ELIAS PEISSNER, *Union College.*

I take great pleasure in recommending Pujol and Van Norman's French Class-Book, as there is no French grammar or class-book which can be compared with it in completeness, system, clearness, and general utility.

From EDWARD NORTH, *President of Hamilton College.*

I have carefully examined Pujol and Van Norman's French Class-Book, and am satisfied of its superiority, for college purposes, over any other heretofore used. We shall not fail to use it with our next class in French.

From A. CURTIS, *Pres't of Cincinnati Literary and Scientific Institute.*

I am confident that it may be made an instrument in conveying to the student, in from six months to a year, the art of speaking and writing the French with almost native fluency and propriety.

From HIRAM ORCUTT, A. M., *Prin. Glenwood and Tilden Ladies' Seminaries.*

I have used Pujol's French Grammar in my two seminaries, exclusively, for more than a year, and have no hesitation in saying that I regard it the best text-book in this department extant. And my opinion is confirmed by the testimony of Prof. F. De Launay and Mademoiselle Marindin. They assure me that the book is eminently accurate and practical, as tested in the school-room.

From PROF. THEO. F. DE FUMAT, *Hebrew Educational Institute, Memphis, Tenn.*

M. Pujol's French Grammar is one of the best and most practical works. The French language is chosen and elegant in style—modern and easy. It is far superior to the other French class-books in this country. The selection of the conversational part is very good, and will interest pupils; and being all completed in only one volume, it is especially desirable to have it introduced in our schools.

From PROF. JAMES H. WORMAN, *Bordentown Female College, N. J.*

The work is upon the same plan as the text-books for the study of French and English published in Berlin, for the study of those who have not the aid of a teacher, and these books are considered, by the first authorities, the best books. In most of our institutions, Americans teach the modern languages, and heretofore the trouble has been to give them a text-book that would dispose of the difficulties of the French pronunciation. This difficulty is successfully removed by P. and Van N., and I have every reason to believe it will soon make its way into most of our best schools.

From PROF. CHARLES S. DOD, *Ann Smith Academy, Lexington, Va.*

I cannot do better than to recommend "Pujol and Van Norman." For comprehensive and systematic arrangement, progressive and thorough development of all grammatical principles and idioms, with a due admixture of theoretical knowledge and practical exercise, I regard it as superior to any (other) book of the kind.

From A. A. FORSTER, *Prin. Pinehurst School, Toronto, C. W.*

I have great satisfaction in bearing testimony to M. Pujol's System of French Instruction, as given in his complete class-book. For clearness and comprehensiveness, adapted for all classes of pupils, I have found it superior to any other work of the kind, and have now used it for some years in my establishment with great success.

From PROF. OTTO FEDDER, *Maplewood Institute, Pittsfield, Mass.*

The conversational exercises will prove an immense saving of the hardest kind of labor to teachers. There is scarcely any thing more trying in the way of teaching language, than to rack your brain for short and easily intelligible bits of conversation, and to repeat them time and again with no better result than extorting at long intervals a doubting "oui," or a hesitating "non, monsieur."

☞ For further testimony of a similar character, see special circular, and current numbers of the Educational Bulletin.

THE CLASSICS.

BROOKS' SERIES.

Brooks' First Lessons in Latin . . . . . .$ 75

Is composed of a regular series of inductive exercises for beginners, and is a Grammar, Reader, and Dictionary combined.

Brooks' Historia Sacra, ... 75

Selections from the Scriptures, in easy Latin, for lower classes. Includes copious notes and a Lexicon, with exercises in Grammar.

Brooks' First Greek Lessons, ... 75

Arranged on the same plan as the author's Latin Lessons.

Brooks' Collectanea Evangelica, ... 75

Selections from the four Gospels, in Greek, forming a connected history of the life of the Saviour. Notes and Lexicon.

Brooks' Ross' Latin Grammar, ... 1 00

A very popular text-book—much improved by Prof. BROOKS' experienced hand.

Brooks' Viri Illustres Americæ, ... 1 50

The lives of illustrious Americans, in Latin, with copious Illustrations, Notes, and Lexicon. The language is used in its purest type, while simple, and adapted to the wants of students not yet prepared for the more difficult construction of classical authors.

Brooks' Cæsar's Commentaries, ... 1 50

The handsomest and most complete annotated edition of any classical author ever published. The volume contains a map of Gaul, Life of Cæsar in English, Table of Epochs, eleven full-page battle plans, countless illustrative engravings, an extended "Argument" prefacing each book, full Notes, References to Andrews & Stoddard's Latin Grammar, and a complete Lexicon—all furnished at as low price as any other edition.

Brooks' Ovid's Metamorphoses 2 50

Possesses all the advantages claimed for the preceding volumes. All objectionable matter is carefully expurgated.

Silber's Latin Course, ... 1 25

A complete work, with Grammar, Reader, Notes, Lexicon, and References to the three leading Latin Grammars—Andrews & Stoddard's, Bullions', and Harkness'.

Dwight's Grecian and Roman Mythology.

School edition, $1 25 ; University edition,*2 25

A knowledge of the fables of antiquity, thus presented in a systematic form, is as indispensable to the student of general literature as to him who would peruse intelligently the classical authors. The mythological allusions so frequent in literature are readily understood with such a Key as this.

Brooks' Latin and Greek Classics.

TESTIMONIALS.

From REV. E. A. DALRYMPLE, *Pres. School of Languages, University of Maryland.*

In the hands of a judicious and pains-taking master, Dr. Brooks' Works furnish all that is necessary for easy and satisfactory progress on sound principles. It appears to me that they are prepared with great care and judgment, and by one who well understands what is required by young people when they begin the rudiments of the classical languages.

From REV. GEO. A. CHASE, A.M., *President Brookville College, Indiana.*

Your Historia Sacra and Greek Lessons are superior to any works of the same class extant.

From BATTISTA LORINO, *Prof. of Languages, Maryland Agricultural College.*

I have carefully examined the Series of Latin and Greek School-Books edited by N. C. Brooks, LL.D., and find them in every respect deserving the attention and commendation of the learned press and of classical scholars. Mr. Brooks' Ovid is generally known among scholars, and is a great favorite with the young. His Cæsar may justly be considered a model text-book; it leaves scarcely any thing to be desired, and is well calculated to supersede every other edition now in use. But Mr. Brooks' laborious, original, and patriotic efforts, to write the lives of illustrious Americans in correct and easy Latin for beginners, deserve more than a passing notice.

From R. G. CHANEY, A.M., *Principal West River Classical Institute.*

We admire the entire arrangement of the work (Viri Americæ) and believe that its tendency is to foster in our youth a love of country from the noble examples of our patriotic sires. We have an interesting class now studying this work, and find that it awakens a new interest; *they study it for the love of it.* A deep interest is felt also by our students in reading his Collectanea Evangelica, embracing the Four Gospels in chronological order. We have also used Dr. Brooks' expurgated Ovid, and consider it the best edition before the public.

From EDWARD SPARKS, A.M., M D., *Prof. Ancient Languages, St. John's College.*

With your revised edition of Ross' Latin Grammar I am much pleased. As a practical proof of my favorable opinion of its merits, I have directed a class to furnish themselves with copies.

From J. R. KINNEY, *Superintendent Schools, Defiance, Ohio.*

Our scholars, and all who have examined Brooks' Cæsar, are very much pleased. The dictionary, the peculiar character of the notes with reference to etymology and syntax, and particularly the illustrations, are all features which recommend it to our warmest approbation. It has been adopted upon its merits.

From the AMERICAN EDUCATIONAL MONTHLY, *New York.*

We think the Cæsar is altogether the finest edition of any classical author, edited for the purposes of elementary instruction, which we have ever seen. * * * * Viri Americæ is a much more practical and available work than those (of similar character—Viri Romæ, Vita Washingtonii, &c.) preceding it. The Latin is simple and pure, and the sketches well written. The book is profusely illustrated with medal portraits of leading men, is printed on tinted paper, and has an excellent lexicon.

From the AMERICAN LITERARY GAZETTE, *Philadelphia.*

Mr. Brooks is qualified by poetic taste for appreciating the beauties of classic writers, and his enthusiasm and industry supply him with the most desirable qualities of an editor. The general merits of his works are well known, and although some of them have been before the public for several years, their hold upon the favor of a large number of teachers is shown by the successive editions that have been called for. The Ovid and the Cæsar are the most laborious performances of the series, and both works are marked by peculiar characteristics of excellence. We do not find that the editor has used his notes as a sort of reservoir into which to empty the results of German erudition. Mr. Brooks strives to beget a study of the text of his author by pointing out the literary beauties, and by furnishing parallelisms from our own literature and the Bible. He would develop not only the mere verbal or grammatical ability, but the rather cultivate the taste and the moral sense by means of classical study. He presses towards the results without stopping midway in the means. In addition to this tendency he aims to give present life to the classics. In the "Vitæ Virorum Illustrium Americæ" we have sketches of our countrymen, in the perusal of which the Latin seems to become a living language; and in thus beholding it dealing with current events, we cease to treat it as altogether a dead thing.

LITERATURE.

THEORY.

Brookfield's First Book in Composition, . . $ 50

Making the cultivation of this important art feasible for the smallest child. By a new method, to induce and stimulate thought.

Boyd's Composition and Rhetoric, ... 1 25

This work furnishes all the aid that is needful or can be desired in the various departments and styles of composition, both in prose and verse.

Day's Art of Rhetoric, ... 1 25

Noted for exactness of definition, clear limitation, and philosophical development of subject; the large share of attention given to Invention, as a branch of Rhetoric, and the unequaled analysis of style.

Boyd's Kames' Criticism, ... 1 75

The best edition of this standard work; without the study of which none may be considered proficient in Belles Lettres.

Walker's Rhyming Dictionary. *1 25

A complete lexicon of allowable rhymes, to aid the composer of rythmical matter.

PRACTICE.

Boyd's Milton's Paradise Lost, ... *1 25

Boyd's Young's Night Thoughts, ... *1 25

Boyd's Cowper's Task, Table Talk, &c., . *1 25

Boyd's Thomson's Seasons, ... *1 25

Boyd's Pollok's Course of Time, ... *1 25

Boyd's Lord Bacon's Essays, ... *1 75

This series of annotated editions of great English writers, in prose and poetry, is designed for critical reading and parsing in schools. Prof. J. R. Boyd proves himself an editor of high capacity, and the works themselves need no encomium. As auxiliary to the study of Composition and Rhetoric these works have no equal.

Pope's Essay on Man, ... *20

Pope's Homer's Iliad, ... *1 00

The metrical translation of the great poet of antiquity, and the matchless "Essay on the Nature and State of Man," by ALEXANDER POPE, afford superior exercise in literature and parsing.

MENTAL PHILOSOPHY.

Mahan's Intellectual Philosophy $1 50

The subject exhaustively considered. The author has evinced learning, candor, and independent thinking.

Mahan's Science of Logic 1 88

A profound analysis of the laws of thought. The system possesses the merit of being intelligible and self-consistent. In addition to the author's carefully elaborated views, it embraces results attained by the ablest minds of Great Britain, Germany, and France, in this department.

Boyd's Elements of Logic 1 00

A systematic and philosophic condensation of the subject, fortified with additions from Watts, Abercrombie, Whateley, &c.

Watts on the Mind 50

The Improvement of the Mind, by Isaac Watts, is designed as a guide for the attainment of useful knowledge. As a text-book it is unparalleled; and the discipline it affords cannot be too highly esteemed by the educator.

MORAL PHILOSOPHY.

Alden's Text-Book of Ethics, ... 60

For young pupils. To aid in systematizing the ethical teachings of the Bible, and point out the coincidences between the instructions of the sacred volume and the sound conclusions of reason.

Willard's Morals for the Young, ...* 60

Lessons in conversational style to inculcate the elements of moral philosophy. The study is made attractive by narratives and engravings.

POLITICAL SCIENCE.

Young Citizen's Catechism 60

Explaining the duties of District, Town, City, County, State, and United States Officers, with rules for parliamentary and commercial business—that which every future "sovereign" ought to know, and so few are taught.

Mansfield's Political Manual 1 25

This is a complete view of the theory and practice of the General and State Governments of the United States, designed as a text-book. The author is an esteemed and able professor of constitutional law, widely known for his sagacious utterances in matters of statecraft through the public press. Recent events teach with emphasis the vital necessity that the rising generation should comprehend the noble polity of the American government, that they may act intelligently when endowed with a voice in it.

TEACHERS' AIDS.

Brooks' School Manual of Devotion . . . 60

This volume contains daily devotional exercises, consisting of a hymn, selections of scripture for alternate reading by teacher and pupils, and a prayer. Its value for opening and closing school is apparent.

Cleaveland's School Harmonist *75

Contains appropriate *tunes* for each hymn in the "Manual of Devotion" described above.

The Boy Soldier 60

Complete infantry tactics for schools, with illustrations, for the use of those who would introduce this pleasing relaxation from the confining duties of the desk.

Welch's Object Lessons *75

Invaluable for teachers of primary schools. Contains the best explanation of the Pestalozzian system. By its aid the proficiency of pupils and the general interest of the school may be increased one hundred per cent.

Tracy's School Record *75

To record attendance, deportment, and scholarship; containing also many useful tables and suggestions to teachers, that are worth of themselves the price of the book.

Tracy's Pocket Record *60

A portable edition of the School Record, without the tables, &c.

Brooks' Teacher's Register . . . .* 90

Presents at one view a record of attendance, recitations, and deportment for the whole term.

Carter's Record and Roll-Book *1 50

For large graded schools.

National School Diary, per dozen *1 25

A little book of blank forms for weekly report of the standing of each scholar, from teacher to parent. A great convenience.

THE

TEACHER'S LIBRARY.

Too many teachers deem that the Normal School or Collegiate training which they may have received before entering upon the active duties of their profession, is all-sufficient preparation for their responsible calling; and, thenceforth, the daily routine of the school-room is to constitute the sole professional exercise that is incumbent upon them. Never was greater mistake. The teacher who is not *progressive* him self, will never send forth scholars who are proficient. Those who have been the most successful, and whose names are honored among all the brotherhood, attribute their success more to personal magnetism—the spirit of "Come, boys!" not "Go, boys!"—than to any other agency which they bring to their task. The student teacher makes student scholars.

The first question which the wide-awake teacher asks himself, after entering upon his duties and properly organizing his school, is, "What course for *self-improvement* can I most advantageously pursue?" and the answer which naturally presents itself—"Avail myself of the experience of those who have preceded me." This is easy, thanks to enterprising men, who have studied and labored, despaired and rejoiced, suffered and reaped their reward in the same paths upon which thousands of new foot-steps enter annually. With a whole-souled love of their profession, and regard for those who pursue it, they have committed their experience and its lessons to the press, so that "he who runs may read."

In no way can teachers so fitly benefit themselves as in the perusal of these volumes, in which they should take a professional pride. Here are the records and results of the life labor of those who have stood highest in the ranks, and who are peculiarly qualified for the task they undertake.

Object Lessons—Welch . . . .$* 75

This is a complete exposition of the popular modern system of "object-teaching," for teachers of primary classes.

Theory and Practice of Teaching—Page .*1 50

This volume has, without doubt, been read by two hundred thousand teachers, and its popularity remains undiminished—large editions being exhausted yearly. It was the pioneer, as it is now the patriarch of professional works for teachers.

The Graded School—Wells *1 25

The proper way to organize graded schools is here illustrated. The author has availed himself of the best elements of the several systems prevalent in Boston, New York, Philadelphia, Cincinnati, St. Louis, and other cities.

The Normal—Holbrook *1 50

Carries a working school on its visit to teachers, showing the most approved methods of teaching all the common branches, including the technicalities, explanations, demonstrations, and definitions introductory and peculiar to each branch.

The Teachers' Institute—Fowle *1 25

This is a volume of suggestions inspired by the author's experience at institutes, in the instruction of young teachers. A thousand points of interest to this class are most satisfactorily dealt with.

The Teacher and the Parent—Northend . $*1 50

A treatise upon common-school education, designed to lead teachers to view their calling in its true light, and to stimulate them to fidelity.

The Teachers' Assistant—Northend *1 50

A natural continuation of the author's previous work, more directly calculated for daily use in the administration of school discipline and instruction.

School Government—Jewell *1 50

Full of advanced ideas on the subject which its title indicates. The criticisms upon current theories of punishment and schemes of administration have excited general attention and comment.

Grammatical Diagrams—Jewell *1 00

The diagram system of teaching grammar explained, defended, and improved. The curious in literature, the searcher for truth, those interested in new inventions, as well as the disciples of Prof. Clark, who would see their favorite theory fairly treated, all want this book. There are many who would like to be made familiar with this system before risking its use in a class. The opportunity is here afforded.

The Complete Examiner—Stone *1 25

Consists of a series of questions on every English branch of school and academic instruction, with reference to a given page or article of leading text-books where the answer may be found in full. Prepared to aid teachers in securing certificates, pupils in preparing for promotion, and teachers in selecting review questions.

School Amusements—Root *1 50

To assist teachers in making the school interesting, with hints upon the management of the school-room. Rules for military and gymnastic exercises are included. Illustrated by diagrams.

Institute Lectures on Mental and Moral Culture—Bates *1 50

These lectures, originally delivered before institutes, are based upon various topics of interest to the teacher. The volume is calculated to prepare the will, awaken the inquiry, and stimulate the thought of the zealous teacher.

Method of Teachers' Institutes—Bates . . . * 75

Sets forth the best method of conducting institutes, with a detailed account of the object, organization, plan of instruction, and true theory of education on which such instruction should be based.

History and Progress of Education *1 50

The systems of education prevailing in all nations and ages, the gradual advance to the present time, and the bearing of the past upon the present in this regard, are worthy of the careful investigation of all concerned in the cause.

American Education—Mansfield $1 50

A treatise on the principles and elements of education, as practiced in this country, with ideas towards distinctive republican and Christian education.

American Institutions—De Tocqueville . .*1 50

A valuable index to the genius of our Government.

Universal Education—Mayhew *1 50

The subject is approached with the clear, keen perception of one who has observed its necessity, and realized its feasibility and expediency alike. The redeeming and elevating power of improved common schools constitutes the inspiration of the volume.

Higher Christian Education—Dwight . . .*1 50

A treatise on the principles and spirit, the modes, directions, and results of all true teaching; showing that right education should appeal to every element of enthusiasm in the teacher's nature.

Modern Philology—Dwight *1 75

Important to the grammarian, and indispensable to the teacher of language, ancient or modern, who would afford his pupils the advantage of the analogy and association to be derived from an intelligent comparison of all languages and their history.

Lectures on Natural History—Chadbourne * 75

Affording many themes for oral instruction in this interesting science—especially in schools where it is not pursued as a class exercise.

Outlines of Mathematical Science—Davies *1 00

A manual suggesting the best methods of presenting mathematical instruction on the part of the teacher, with that comprehensive view of the whole which is necessary to the intelligent treatment of a part, in science.

Logic & Utility of Mathematics—Davies . .*1 50

An elaborate and lucid exposition of the principles which lie at the foundation of pure mathematics, with a highly ingenious application of their results to the development of the essential idea of the different branches of the science.

Mathematical Dictionary—Davies & Peck . 3 75

This cyclopædia of mathematical science defines with completeness, precision, and accuracy, every technical term, thus constituting a popular treatise on each branch, and a general view of the whole subject.

School Architecture—Barnard 2 25

Attention is here called to the vital connection between a good schoolhouse and a good school, with plans and specifications for securing the former in the most economical and satisfactory manner.

THE SCHOOL LIBRARY.

The two elements of instruction and entertainment were never more happily combined than in this collection of standard books. Children and adults alike will here find ample food for the mind, of the sort that is easily *digested*, while not degenerating to the level of modern romance.

LIBRARY OF LITERATURE.

Milton's Paradise Lost Boyd's Illustrated Ed. $1 75

Young's Night Thoughts . . . . do. . . 1 75

Cowper's Task, Table Talk, &c. . do. . . 1 75

Thomson's Seasons . . . . . . do. . . 1 75

Pollok's Course of Time . . . . do. . . 1 75

These great moral poems are known wherever the English language is read, and are regarded as models of the best and purest literature. The books are beautifully illustrated, and notes explain all doubtful meanings, and furnish other matter of interest to the general reader.

Lord Bacon's Essays, (Boyd's Edition.) . . . 1 75

Another grand English classic, affording the highest example of purity in language and style.

The Iliad of Homer. Translated by Pope. . . 1 00

Those who are unable to read this greatest of ancient writers in the original, should not fail to avail themselves of this metrical version by an eminent scholar and poet.

The Poets of Connecticut—Everest 1 75

With the biographical sketches, this volume forms a complete history of the poetical literature of the State.

The Son of a Genius—Hofland 75

A juvenile classic which never wears out, and finds many interested readers in every generation of youth.

Lady Willoughby 1 00

The diary of a wife and mother, An historical romance of the seventeenth century. At once beautiful and pathetic, entertaining and instructive.

The Rhyming Dictionary—Walker 1 25

A serviceable manual to composers of rhythmical matter, being a complete index of allowable rhymes.

LIBRARY OF REFERENCE.

Home Cyclopædia of Chronology $2 25

An index to the sources of knowledge—a dictionary of dates.

Home Cyclopædia of Geography 2 25

A complete gazetteer of the world.

Home Cyclopædia of Useful Arts 2 25

Covering the principles and practice of modern scientific enterprise, with a record of important inventions in agriculture, architecture, domestic economy, engineering, machinery, manufactures, mining, photogenic and telegraphic art, &c., &c.

Home Cyclopædia of Literature & Fine Arts 2 25

A complete index to all terms employed in belles lettres, philosophy, theology, law, mythology, painting, music, sculpture, architecture, and all kindred arts.

LIBRARY OF TRAVEL.

Ship and Shore—Colton 1 50

In Madeira, Lisbon, and the Mediterranean Ocean. Illustrated.

Land and Lee—Colton 1 50

In the Bosphorus and Ægean. Illustrated.

Sea and Sailor—Colton 1 50

Notes on France and Italy. Illustrated.

Deck and Port—Colton 1 50

A cruise to California. Illustrated.

Three Years in California—Colton 1 50

During the gold fever. Illustrated.

These racy descriptions of travel are regarded as models in this department of literature. They are read by old and young with vast interest and profit.

A Visit to Europe—Silliman, 2 vols. 3 00

A very spicy book of foreign travel. It brings every opportunity of the tourist to the feet of the reader.

TRAVEL—Continued.

Life in the Sandwich Islands—Cheever . .$1 50

The "heart of the Pacific, as it was and is," shows most vividly the contrast between the depth of degradation and barbarism, and the light and liberty of civilization, so rapidly realized in these islands under the humanizing influence of the Christian religion. Illustrated.

Peruvian Antiquities—Von Tschudi 1 50

Travels in Peru—Von Tschudi 1 50

The first of these volumes affords whatever information has been attained by travelers and men of science concerning the extinct people who once inhabited Peru, and who have left behind them many relics of a wonderful civilization. The "Travels" furnish valuable information concerning the country and its inhabitants as they now are. Illustrated.

Ancient Monasteries of the East—Curzon . 1 50

The exploration of these ancient seats of learning has thrown much light upon the researches of the historian, the philologist, and the theologian, as well as the general student of antiquity. Illustrated.

Discoveries in Babylon & Nineveh—Layard 1 75

Valuable alike for the information imparted with regard to these most interesting ruins, and the pleasant adventures and observations of the author in regions that to most men seem like Fairyland. Illustrated.

Egypt and the Holy Land—Spencer . . . 1 75

Still another volume of eastern travel. The many incontrovertible proofs of Scripture observed by the pains-taking modern traveler are worth the price of the book. Illustrated.

St. Petersburgh—Jermann 1 00

Americans are less familiar with the history and social customs of the Russian people than those of any other modern civilized nation. Opportunities such as this book affords are not, therefore, to be neglected.

The Polar Regions—Osborn 1 25

A thrilling and intensely interesting narrative of one of the famous expeditions in search of Sir John Franklin—unsuccessful in its main object, but adding many facts to the repertoire of science.

Thirteen Months in the Confederate Army 75

The author, a northern man conscripted into the Confederate service, and rising from the ranks by soldierly conduct to positions of responsibility, had remarkable opportunities for the acquisition of facts respecting the conduct of the Southern armies, and the policy and deeds of their leaders. He participated in many engagements, and his book is one of the most exciting narratives of adventure ever published. Mr. Stevenson takes no ground as a partizan, but views the whole subject as with the eye of a neutral—only interested in subserving the ends of history by the contribution of impartial facts. Illustrated.

www.ingramcontent.com/pod-product-compliance
Lightning Source LLC
LaVergne TN
LVHW010227110826
845151LV00004B/1206

* 9 7 8 1 4 2 5 5 2 5 7 9 8 *